"Drawing from his years of expe [barcode] ep-
herded countless patients throug th,'
John Dunlop provides pastoral w *ing
Well to the Glory of God is filled with examples from and
practice, laced with rich Scriptures, and punctuated with thoughtful
prayers. Dr. Dunlop gently addresses spiritual, emotional, psychological,
financial, and physical needs. This book helps us plan our final decades,
months, weeks, and hours with a God-centered attitude toward death
and dying."

> **Paige Cunningham,** Executive Director, The Center for
> Bioethics and Human Dignity

"Anyone who thinks the Bible is archaic will be quickly dissuaded after
reading Dr. Dunlop's scriptural insights. To these insights he adds his
professional observations, personal stories, and very practical advice.
The strategies he offers are clearly the result of years of experience in
caring, deeply caring, for persons in their twilight years. This book will
be helpful for patients and families both before death and afterward."

> **Robert Orr,** Distinguished Fellow, The Center for Bioethics &
> Human Dignity

"This volume by John Dunlop is a brilliant combination of biblical
reflection, medical expertise, and godly, warm-hearted wisdom. This
book will be of great help to those who are approaching the end of
their lives as well as all who want to prepare now to finish well in the
future. Friends, family members, and other caregivers will benefit from
Dunlop's wisdom. I was especially moved by his discussion of completing
the agenda of our lives and of the decision-making process of changing
gears from cure to comfort. May God give this book a wide hearing!"

> **Steve Roy,** Associate Professor of Pastoral Theology,
> Trinity Evangelical Divinity School

"Don't face your death or that of a loved one unprepared. *Finishing Well*
is the most comprehensive, deeply Christian, and readable resource I
know of its kind, and it will prepare you and your loved ones to die well."

> **David Stevens, MD, CEO,** Christian Medical and
> Dental Association

"Here is a practical guide, brimming with the fresh wisdom of medical experience, a pervasive God-centered vision, and a deft pastoral touch reminiscent of the Puritan divines. John Dunlop has done the church a great service in this book, probing very difficult questions that all people, not least Christians, must face as physical death approaches. Christians in the West can be doubly grateful since they, of all believers worldwide, are culturally least equipped on these matters. Just to consume the many stories, lessons learned, and anecdotes laid out in these pages, each one betraying years of keen observation, is a lavish meal and worth the price of the book. Dunlop offers a compelling guide for us all as we prepare to finish well—to die—to the glory of God. Sell your shirt and buy a copy for all your friends and family!"

> **Hans Madueme,** Assistant Professor of Theological Studies,
> Covenant College

"Who would not want love, hope, and joy at the end of life? But how does one gain them? What Christian would not welcome letting go, growing through adversity, and resting in Jesus? But how does one experience them? Dr. John Dunlop provides extremely practical and well-tested answers to these and other equally vital questions. Anyone facing death or expecting to do so someday will be wonderfully blessed by this book."

> **John Kilner,** Forman Chair of Christian Ethics and Theology,
> Trinity Evangelical Divinity School

"Dunlop is the doctor we all want: clever, wise, faithful, and motivated by clear Christian values. If you need to think about aging and death—and we all do—you couldn't do better than this book."

> **Josh Moody,** Senior Pastor, College Church, Wheaton, Illinois

FINISHING WELL
to the
GLORY *of*
GOD

FINISHING
WELL
to the
GLORY *of*
GOD

STRATEGIES from a CHRISTIAN PHYSICIAN

JOHN DUNLOP, MD

CROSSWAY®

WHEATON, ILLINOIS

Finishing Well to the Glory of God: Strategies from a Christian Physician
Copyright © 2011 by John Dunlop
Published by Crossway
         1300 Crescent Street
         Wheaton, Illinois 60187

All rights reserved. No part of this publication may be reproduced, stored in a retrieval system, or transmitted in any form by any means, electronic, mechanical, photocopy, recording, or otherwise, without the prior permission of the publisher, except as provided for by USA copyright law. Crossway® is a registered trademark in the United States of America.

Interior design and typesetting: Lakeside Design Plus
Cover design: Dual Identity inc.
Cover photo: iStock
First printing 2011
Printed in the United States of America

Unless otherwise indicated, Scripture quotations are from the ESV® Bible (The Holy Bible, English Standard Version®), copyright © 2001 by Crossway, a publishing ministry of Good News Publishers. Used by permission. All rights reserved.

Scripture references marked NIV are from the HOLY BIBLE, NEW INTERNATIONAL VERSION®. Copyright © 1973, 1978, 1984 Biblica. Used by permission of Zondervan. All rights reserved. The "NIV" and "New International Version" trademarks are registered in the United States Patent and Trademark Office by Biblica. Use of either trademark requires the permission of Biblica.

Trade Paperback ISBN: 978-1-4335-1347-3
PDF ISBN: 978-1-4335-1348-0
Mobipocket ISBN: 978-1-4335-1349-7
ePub ISBN: 978-1-4335-2413-4

Library of Congress Cataloging-in-Publication Data
Dunlop, John, 1947–
Finishing well to the glory of God : strategies from a Christian physician / John Dunlop.
    p. cm.
  Includes bibliographical references (p.   ).
  ISBN 978-1-4335-1347-3 (tp)
  1. Death—Religious aspects—Christianity. I. Title.
BT825.D785   2011
248.8'6—dc22   2010036246

Crossway is a publishing ministry of Good News Publishers.

CH   26   25   24   23   22   21   20   19   18   17   16

To Dorothy
A Gift of God to Me

Contents

Introduction

Jeb would have been considered a Christian statesman. Having realized God's great love for him at an early age, he had learned that his greatest passion was allowing God to be glorified. He had been a leader in his church and founder of a major international Christian mission. But he had been a diabetic for many years, and over his last five years he developed severe heart disease. Jeb had bypass surgery twice, and decided not to go through it again. He knew that he had lived a full life, but that soon God would call him home. Jeb had begun to let go of his attachments to his life and was longing to see his Lord in heaven. One Sunday he was admitted to intensive care with a major heart attack. By Monday afternoon it was clear that he was dying. I went to see him that evening. Upon reviewing his status, I told him that his heart was failing rapidly and he would not likely live out the night. Thankfully, he was fully alert and coherent. His response was unforgettable. He took my hand and said, "John, thank you for being so candid. I would like to ask for three things. First, the visiting policies of this hospital stink. My wife and daughters are

11

in the waiting room, and I would like them to come back here with me—now! Second, as you know, I have been a diabetic for many years and I have watched my diet, but could you get me a piece of chocolate cake with chocolate icing? Third, I have not been able to have a cup of real coffee for some time and wonder if you would let me have one." With tears in my eyes, I agreed to all of his requests. His family came right in. He fully enjoyed his cake and coffee, and shortly after finishing them he said good-bye to his wife and daughters, laid his head on his pillow, and died. There was no fight to the finish; he simply rested in Jesus. He had lived his life for God's glory, and he came to the end of life to the glory of God.

I later saw a cartoon that will be forever imprinted on my mind. It showed an older fellow walking up to the pearly gates with a tube hanging from every orifice of his body. His comment to St. Peter was, "Sorry I'm late, but they kept me on life support for two weeks!" The point was well made.

I have practiced internal medicine for over thirty years with a special interest in geriatrics. As a result I sign a lot of death certificates. As I do the paperwork, I do some reflecting. I ask myself, Was this a good death? Were we aggressive enough? Or were we too aggressive? Was the patient prepared? Was the family ready? Because I have had the privilege of taking care of many like Jeb who had faith in Jesus, I have pondered other questions, such as, Is there a distinctively Christian way to come to the end of life? How do we finish well to the glory of God, assuring that death is an affirmation of faith, consistent with the gospel? These are critical questions, ones which we would do well to consider.

One thing I have learned is that dying well is rarely a coincidence. Rather it results from choices made throughout life. After all, dying well is nothing more than living well right up till the end. Deliberate planning for our final days is not a priority of our culture. But we need it today more than ever. The way we approach the end of life is rapidly changing. We are often forced to make difficult medical decisions during times of crisis. Many of the options we have available now would have been science fiction less than a generation ago. It is impossible to anticipate what specific situations we will face down the line, but our values will determine whatever decisions we come to. It has been my experience that if we carefully think through the values that will inform future choices, we will spare ourselves and our loved ones the risk of making wrong decisions under duress. One of my goals, for you who read this book, is to help you define the values that will determine your approach to the dilemmas you will face toward the end of life. I trust that you will come to understand that the greatest value we can have is that God ought to be glorified.

The realities of modern medicine present potential problems of two sorts: choosing too much of the available technology or choosing too little. If we are unduly aggressive at the end of life, death, instead of being a peaceful resting in Jesus, will become a technological fight to the finish. On the other hand, if we forgo what could be truly effective interventions, we may not prove to be good caretakers of the life God has entrusted to us. This is particularly true when we are faced with the possibilities of physician-assisted suicide and euthanasia. Clearly we need balance. We should pursue treatment, when possible, to honor life. Yet, we should not resist God when it appears that he has willed life to end.

These issues have prompted me to think a lot about how to help my patients prepare to finish life well. I realized some time ago that the amount of material I would have to share with them was much more than I could cover in an office visit; it would actually fill a whole book. That is what led me to write *Finishing Well to the Glory of God*. I write this book from several perspectives. First, I write as a Christian, and the longer I live, the more convinced I am that God alone is the source of all true joy and fulfillment. Second, I write as a physician; third, as a son who has seen his parents go through their later days; and finally I write as a cancer survivor who in his sixties is confronting some of the issues of aging myself.

Strategies from a Christian Physician

Finishing Well to the Glory of God is written from an explicitly Christian perspective. Here I need to make three comments.

First, while being a book *about* Christians, this is not exclusively a book *for* Christians. If one is considering the validity of the Christian faith, it is essential to reflect on a Christian view of the end of life. Christianity, after all, is the only major world religion based on the death of its founder. Yet it is not Christ's death but the fact that he rose from the dead that gives his followers a uniquely triumphant view of the end of life. For the Christian, death is not so much an end but a beginning. I have embraced this hope for most of my life. It is, therefore, difficult for me to put myself in the intellectual position of a non-Christian. But, if I were doing an honest investigation in the marketplace of the world's religions, I would first want to examine their bases for claiming to be true. Then, I would want to know how the religion would help me not only to live but also to die. Finally, I would want to consider what sort of experience the religion promised after death.

Christianity tells adherents that death leads a believer immediately into the presence of God with the expectation of a continued relationship with many of the things and people enjoyed on earth. Furthermore, followers of Jesus can know their eternal future with surety before death, for entrance into heaven is not based upon good works but upon what Jesus accomplished when he died in their place. A Christian has stopped trying to earn God's favor and is simply willing to accept what Jesus has done. Most impressively, Christianity teaches that the relationship we will experience with God for all of eternity will fulfill the deepest longings of our beings. This is not the extinction of desire as so many Eastern religions teach but its fulfillment. If you do not consider yourself a Christian, this book will be valuable because many of the strategies apply whether you are a Christian or not, and it will allow you to evaluate basic Christian beliefs about life and death.

A second thought about my Christian perspective is that I do not claim dogmatically that my application of Christian truth is the only one. Many of the issues I write about are far too complex, and the latitude we find in the Bible is far too broad, for me to claim to have the only approach to the end of life. I believe though, that my approach is consistent with biblical truth and can be practically applied in the complex medical world we face today.

A third comment is that I understand and appreciate that there are cultural biases on these issues. My background would be categorized as white, middle class, and suburban. Though I have sought to reach into the city and to cultivate deep friendships in the African-American and Asian communities, I am still keenly aware of my biases. I have tried to distinguish those opinions that are truly Christian from those that are merely cultural.

Sources

God has graciously given me a number of sources from which I have learned these strategies.

First, my patients: I have had the joy of serving a host of amazing people over the years. Many have been Christians, others have not. I have seen many die well from both groups. They have shown courage and kindness in the face of death. You will read many of their stories. I have altered names and many details to protect their anonymity. In some instances I tell an anecdote that is a composite of several stories. Some of the histories are hypothetical.

Second, but most important, the Scriptures: in them I find truth and wisdom. I quote them freely, but I do so committed to the fact that any passage of Scripture must be read and studied in the context of the whole. It is dangerous when we think our own good thoughts and then turn to the Scriptures to prove our point. I try not to do that, intending instead to have my thinking flow out of the wisdom of the whole Bible. It is my intention to use the biblical quotes as examples, not just as a means of proving my point.

Third are a host of authors and friends who began wrestling with these issues long before I did. Some are theologians, some medical professionals, all of them very wise people. I have attempted to give them credit when I cite specific material, but I acknowledge that it is not possible to give due recognition for the little things I have picked up along the way. One person I particularly want to recognize is Charles Sell. "Chick" is a retired seminary professor and experienced writer who holds a doctorate in Systematic Theology. After reviewing some of my notes, he befriended me and generously offered to assist in my writing. Chick has made numerous contributions to most of these strategies. In particular he wrote the sections on grief in strategy 2 and appendix 3. The other individual who deserves special appreciation is Tara Davis, on behalf of Crossway, who has carefully edited this manuscript.

Finishing Well to the Glory of God
Before I introduce the strategies to finish life well, I need to explain what I mean by the phrase "finishing well." Some say it means being happy, pain free, and contented throughout life. Many desire to maintain their dignity and to have enjoyable times with their families and loved ones. These are reasonable goals, but Scripture presents a uniquely Christian approach to the end of life. Consider this:

> As it is my eager expectation and hope that I will not be at all ashamed, but that with full courage now as always Christ will be honored in my body, whether by life or by death. For to me to live is Christ, and to die is gain. (Phil. 1:20–21)

Paul, the apostle, had a God-centered view of life. He longed for God to be honored in his life right up to the end. Upon death he looked forward to being in God's presence, where he knew that Christ would be honored all the more.[1] Finishing life well means that God is glorified in our lives till the moment of our deaths and then by the legacy we leave behind.

Overview of Strategies
A summary of the nine strategies will enable you to appreciate the end-of-life issues we deal with and help you sense the impor-

tance of preparing to face them. Each strategy begins with a list of questions designed to prime your thinking before you read. If you are in a group and discussing *Finishing Well* together, these questions may serve to kick off your discussion.

Strategy 1: Live Well

Finishing Well begins with advice on how to live life well near the end. I encourage you to recognize your God-given value while keeping your focus on serving others and maintaining your health.

Strategy 2: Let Go Graciously

This strategy explains how to let go of some of the things and values of this world in order to more fully embrace eternal life. I try to be sensitive, recognizing how difficult some of these transitions are. I discuss the essential role of hope as we face the end of life, emphasizing that our hope must be in God and not in this world.

Strategy 3: Treasure God's Love; Love Him in Return

In this section, I demonstrate how having an inner experience of God's love will result in a passion for God and godliness as well as a longing for heaven and our resurrected bodies. This longing will transform our attitudes toward the end of life. I show how Christians can have the ultimate joy they were designed to experience.

Strategy 4: Grow through Adversity

This chapter explains how suffering, far from being meaningless, can be productive. It helps us understand a God-centered perspective on some of the challenges of the end of life including pain, suffering, and dementia.

Strategy 5: Embrace a Biblical View of Life and Death

A biblical view of life is much more than our existence here on earth. Death is not a part of God's original good creation but is at root a punishment for sin. It is therefore an enemy. But now it can be a defeated one—one that God uses to lead a Christian to eternal reward.

Strategy 6: Complete Your Agenda

Dying slowly gives an opportunity to strengthen your relationship with God and seek closure with loved ones. I offer an agenda of things you can do to allow closure with your loved ones and to leave a legacy of godliness.

Strategy 7: Make Appropriate Use of Technology

Medical technology is a gracious gift from God that allows us to improve and prolong our lives. But it raises tough questions. In this strategy I provide practical guidelines for choosing whether to pursue aggressive life-sustaining treatment.

Strategy 8: Changing Gears from Cure to Comfort Care

There will come a point when it is appropriate to change the goal of medical care from cure to comfort care, accepting that death will come. This chapter answers the why, when, and how questions that are so difficult. I also discuss advance directives.

Strategy 9: Rest in Jesus

After proper physical, emotional, and spiritual preparation, death need not be a fight to the finish but a gentle resting in the arms of the Savior as we finally yield complete control to him. But death is not always easy; at times it is nasty and ugly. This strategy helps prepare us for a more difficult end.

❧ ❧

Finishing Well concludes with three appendices. The first presents my views on how to maintain health, the second gives guidelines needed when considering specific life-sustaining treatments, and the third advises survivors who must make many decisions while dealing with their own grief.

An Admission

In writing these strategies I am trying to idealize some complex issues and situations. Without doubt the end of life can be very difficult. It may sound from this book that I have always handled things well. I have not. I have made, and continue to make, my share of mistakes. As they say, I am still *practicing* medicine.

Prayer

Even though it is difficult to think about end-of-life issues, I am reminded of what Moses wrote: "So teach us to number our days that we may get a heart of wisdom" (Ps. 90:12). My prayer is that as you reflect on the later days of your life, you will live wisely and recognize your need for God's help in your decisions. I pray that you will have God's wisdom as you approach your later years, allowing you to finish well. I encourage you to pray for God's help after you read each strategy. I have included a brief sample prayer with each one. Reflecting on the reasons we as Christians can finish well should also lead us to worship. To facilitate that, I have closed each chapter with a meditation to draw out your heart to God.

I wrote *Finishing Well* with the words of the apostle Paul constantly on my mind: "For from him and through him and to him are all things. To him be glory forever. Amen" (Rom. 11:36). My desire is that, after reading this book, you will recognize God as the origin, means, and goal of your life, and then perhaps "finishing well to the glory of God" will itself be numbered in the "all things" that bring him glory.

Live Well

What are the good aspects of growing older?

What purpose can my life have when I am older?

How do I build deeper friendships?

Are there steps I can take to assure better health?

What things detract from finishing life well?

Finishing life well is living well—right up to the end. Sure, we will always be aware that somewhere out there death is looming, but life is not fundamentally about dying, it is about living.

As a gerontologist, I have many patients who come to the office for a physical exam prior to retirement. I frequently inquire as to their plans and ask them if I can share two rules for retirement. I have never been refused. They are simple:

Rule 1: Wake up every morning knowing what you are going to do that day.

Rule 2: Go to bed every night knowing that you helped someone.

If we think that retirement is a time to sit around and do whatever we please, or if we think that the time has finally come for us to focus on ourselves, we will be miserable and make life so for everyone around us. Ignoring these two rules can lead to depression and even to an early death. Without any meaningful reasons to live, we may experience what commentator Paul Harvey quipped: "Retirement is just practicing up to be dead."[1] While this appears to be true for some people, it is not so for all.

At age ninety-five, Carrie was certainly not "practicing up to be dead." She was one of many delightful elderly women I have been privileged to know. After being independent for twenty years following her husband's death, her family thought it wise for her to give up driving and move out of her home of seventy years to an assisted-living facility. I asked how she felt about all of these changes. Her response was, "I hated giving up visiting the old people at the old folk's home."

Fred was almost the opposite. Though he too was ninety-five, he did not have Carrie's attitude. Sitting in his nursing home bed, he responded to my encouragement by saying, "What's the use? I'm ready to die." I reminded him that there were only two kinds of people: those who are living and those who are dead. I told him, "Unless you are dead, you are still living, so let's get on with it. If you are to come to the end of your life well, it will be much more about how you lived these days than how you died." He had a change of heart and was able to live out his days contentedly at home with his wife and loved ones.

Prescriptions for Finishing Life Well

In this chapter we are not going to focus on the *problems* of the end of life but rather on the *opportunities* it offers. To do this I offer the following prescriptions:

1. Recognize your God-given value.
2. Find purpose for each day.

3. Cultivate and maintain deep friendships.
4. Laugh a lot.
5. Invest in your health.
6. Avoid the things that rob quality from the older years.

Unfortunately, we don't naturally follow these guidelines. To do so requires deliberate planning.

Recognize Your God-Given Value

My friend in the nursing home had no motivation to get up and get going because he failed to appreciate his value.

In our youth-oriented culture, aging is feared, something to be put off as long as possible. It has been said: "Everyone wants to live a long time, but no one wants to grow old." Our culture values youth, physical beauty, and athletic prowess but does not place much value on the elderly. As persons grow old, they become less like what society most esteems.

Contrast this view of the elderly with that of Scripture. A classic passage is in Leviticus: "You shall stand up before the gray head and honor the face of an old man, and you shall fear your God: I am the LORD" (Lev. 19:32). This strong statement affirms that as we honor the elderly, we are showing reverence for God. Appreciate the significance of this statement: "Gray hair is a crown of glory; it is gained in a righteous life" (Prov. 16:31).

In an insightful book, *Growing Old in Christ*, Richard and Judith Hays summarize well the biblical view of the elderly:

> Nowhere in the biblical canon are they pitied, patronized, or treated with condescension. Nowhere is growing old itself described as a problem. Nowhere are elders described as pitiable, irrelevant, or behind the curve, as inactive or unproductive. Nowhere are they, as in so many Western dramas and narratives, lampooned as comic figures.[2]

It's crucial that we cling to the biblical, not the contemporary, view of the elderly. If we do otherwise, we may compromise our own future. If in your younger years you feel that life for the elderly is of little value, chances are you will devalue your own life as you get older. Many seniors respond to aging by continually trying to be young. I've seen ads for senior living facilities showing a group out on the ski slopes. There's nothing wrong with such a vigorous picture of life at that age—unless it forces the elderly to deny who they really are and pretend to be something they are not. Our culture's failure to value the aged is pervasive; I have found myself unthinkingly caught up in it. In years gone by I would congratulate ninety-year-olds for appearing to be only sixty. They would always smile and accept it as a compliment. Then, when I came to realize that by doing so I was implying there was something wrong with being (and looking) ninety, I stopped saying such things.

Rather than deprecating age, we ought to recognize the benefits of growing older, seeing old age as being chronologically gifted rather than chronologically challenged. Wisdom is one of those benefits: "Wisdom is with the aged, and understanding in length of days" (Job 12:12). Granted, young people can be wise and older ones can be foolish. But Scripture validates a certain kind of wisdom that only comes through years of experience. Wisdom is not the same as knowledge. Knowledge is an accumulation of facts. Wisdom is the ability to use well the knowledge we have. It includes the ability to set priorities, to assess value, and to see things in larger perspective. If we want knowledge in today's world, we can surf the Internet, but unfortunately that does not buy us wisdom.

Whether we are young, middle-aged, or elderly ourselves, we need to affirm the value of the elderly.

Find Purpose for Each Day

Those who trust in God should never view any season of life as unproductive, even the last stage. So, wrote the psalmist:

> The righteous flourish like the palm tree
>   and grow like a cedar in Lebanon.
> They are planted in the house of the LORD;
>   they flourish in the courts of our God.
> They still bear fruit in old age;
>   they are ever full of sap and green. (Ps. 92:12–14)

In this passage the godly are characterized by endless vigor. The older years are a time for accomplishment, not a time to sit back and relax. They are an opportunity to do spiritual work. The adage "carpe diem" (seize the day) pertains to all ages. Remember my second rule for retirement: "Go to bed every night knowing that you helped someone." God has a purpose for you to fulfill each day of your life. As we age, however, his purpose for us will undoubtedly change. I may not be serving at my office, giving lectures, or writing books. I may be less involved in things that require physical strength and more committed to quieter activities like praying and encouraging others. Those activities may be more important in God's eternal kingdom than the things I am currently doing. As members of Christ's church we are to be involved in its mission. As part of the body of Christ we are to do his work in the world. That does not mean we need to continue to work at our vocation or even that we need to have a paying job. None of the Bible's commands that tell us to serve are age specific. We read about all believers having spiritual gifts.[3] That surely includes the elderly.

Consider how the apostle Paul viewed his life:

> For to me to live is Christ, and to die is gain. If I am to live in the flesh, that means fruitful labor for me. Yet which I shall choose I cannot tell. I am hard pressed between the two. My desire is to depart and be with Christ, for that is far better. But to remain in the flesh is more necessary on your account. Convinced of this, I know that I will remain and continue with you all, for your progress and joy in the faith, so that in me you may have ample cause to glory in Christ Jesus, because of my coming to you again. (Phil. 1:21–26)

Facing execution at the hands of Nero, Paul had no idea how long he would live. He wrestled with a basic quandary: was he to hope to go on living, or should he hope to die soon and go to be with his Lord? He chose to hope to go on living because he saw purpose in doing so. His remaining days would be spent encouraging the Philippian Christians in their spiritual walk.

Paul displayed the same attitude in 1 Corinthians 15 where he wrote concerning the resurrection of the body. He longed for this new body which he would have in heaven, freed from the constraints of his deteriorating physical health and strength. He described in glowing terms the resurrection that lay ahead for believers. Yet he did not conclude that we should idle away our lives dreaming of this glorious future. Instead, he challenged, "Therefore, my beloved brothers, be steadfast, immovable, always abounding in the work of the Lord, knowing that in the Lord your labor is not in vain" (1 Cor. 15:58).

The apostle Peter laid down the same challenge, even when writing to people who were suffering. To them he wrote: "Therefore let those who suffer according to God's will entrust their souls to a faithful Creator while doing good" (1 Pet. 4:19). Realizing that their suffering was not an accident but according to God's will, they were to put themselves in God's hands and through their suffering learn more about his faithfulness. In addition, they were to "continue to do good"! That life was tough did not excuse them from being out on the front lines serving the Lord.

Joni Eareckson Tada, herself paralyzed, has helped others see that no matter how desperate our situation, we must find some purpose in continuing to live. She spoke by telephone to a young woman who was severely debilitated and confined to bed: "What purpose can I possibly have?" the young woman asked Joni. Without hesitation, Joni answered. Having found that the young woman knew many Scriptures by memory, Joni suggested she could quote passages of the Bible to others. "You can encourage those who visit you or those you speak to on the phone. . . . Besides this," Tada continued, "you can offer others an opportunity to serve and encourage you."[4]

I am often asked to speak to groups of younger Christians about the issues of aging. I frequently ask those in the audience who had been significantly impacted in their spiritual lives by a grandparent or another senior to raise their hands. I am always impressed with how many hands go up. I remember my own grandmother repeatedly reminding me of one verse from the Old Testament: "For those who honor me I will honor . . ." (1 Sam. 2:30).

The Bible is replete with illustrations of seniors making significant contributions, some very near the end of their lives. At age eighty, Moses led the people of Israel from Egypt to the Promised Land. Then there were Abraham and Sarah who, well past the reproductive years, gave birth to their son Isaac. King David made preparations for Solomon to build the temple just prior to his death. Elizabeth, married to an aging Zacharias, gave birth to John the Baptist. Anna and Simeon were at the temple to welcome the predicted Messiah. The apostle John received the Revelation of Jesus Christ when he was over ninety years old.

Perhaps the greatest example of doing good as the end of life approaches is that of our Lord Jesus himself. In the last days of his life he met with his disciples, served them by washing their feet, and instituted the Lord's Supper. In the garden he healed the ear of the High Priest's servant. From the cross he provided for his mother and offered forgiveness to his assailants. Jesus was not focused on his own suffering but considered the needs of others.

Unfortunately, as motivated as some people are to continue to serve others in their later years, they are simply unable to do much. For physical, mental, emotional, or even spiritual reasons, many are limited. When we encounter others facing such limitations, we who are active and involved should be slow to criticize. What is important is that they are serving to the limit of their capabilities. They may be expending more of their maximal capacity than others who seem to accomplish much more.

For as long as God gives us life and abilities, he has a purpose for us to fulfill each day. It is simply our job to find it and to make sure that we are living for Christ and his kingdom.

Cultivate and Maintain Deep Friendships

In younger days we may value activity more than relationships. What we have done, what we are presently doing, and what we intend to do will often define our identity and reflect our values. As we age, we tend to value these activities less and our relationships more. I was impressed that as my dad got older, he talked less about his accomplishments and more about his children, his wife, and his friends. By doing so, he was demonstrating a much wiser and perhaps more biblical value system. After all, as one of my good friends frequently remarks, "People are the only things on earth that God will take to heaven."

Family is often the main source of satisfying relationships. As we age, we must take particular care to nurture close loving relationships with our family. The adage "Be nice to your kids for they will choose your nursing home" has a grain of truth in it. But far beyond the benefits to you will be the legacy that you can leave your children and grandchildren. Nevertheless, family relationships are not enough. We need to cultivate deep friendships within our peer group. Studies have documented a mortality benefit for seniors who maintain deep friendships.[5] I love to see a group of four men (all of whom are my patients) meeting daily for coffee at the local McDonald's "solving the problems of the world." It is not wise for couples to do all of their socializing with themselves or with other couples. When one of them is gone, the survivor needs an established support group.

Christians should build their friendships on the biblical idea of fellowship (often translated from the Greek word *koinonia* in the New Testament), which presents a picture of meaningful interdependence and involvement in the lives of one another. Paul is explicit in what he meant by this when he wrote to the Galatians: "Bear one another's burdens, and so fulfill the law of Christ" (Gal. 6:2). Note this is a command, not a suggestion.

For believers, much of this deep fellowship should take place in small groups within a church. Many churches have groups that help promote fellowship specifically among seniors. If your church does not have this type of group, you may want to consider starting one. You may also choose to develop deep friendships with those who are not Christians.

Bible studies for seniors abound. These are splendid ways not only to provide a social outlet but also to encourage the saints in their walks with the Lord. I am impressed every Sunday night when I talk to my eighty-nine-year-old mother about how she is preparing for her Bible study the next morning, which she attends with other residents of her retirement community. I often meet friends for breakfast at a restaurant near the hospital where I start my workday. Two mornings a week I see a group of seniors from the community gather there for a time of Bible study. Some of the group leaders are seniors themselves, but others are younger people. They are all doing a great service.

As I observe my older friends, I also see the necessity of developing friendships across generational lines. Younger people need the wisdom and support of the elderly, and the elderly need the energy and opportunity to serve the younger. I do not believe that the trend in many churches to isolate the elderly to their own peer group is healthy. The psalmist agreed:

> Young men and maidens together,
>   old men and children!
>
> Let them praise the name of the LORD,
>   for his name alone is exalted;
>   his majesty is above earth and heaven. (Ps. 148:12–13)

Our church puts a great emphasis on small groups. Most of them include people of similar age. However, at least once a quarter we have a social activity that crosses all generational boundaries. That is good.

Relationships contribute a lot to the quality of our lives in the later years. We need to keep that in mind when we have to face difficult choices in our later years. These include our living situation and how we spend our time. We must choose our friendships carefully and cultivate them well.

Laugh a Lot

It's healthy for seniors to laugh and enjoy life with good friends. Ecclesiastes encourages "a time to weep, and a time to laugh; a time to mourn, and a time to dance" (Eccles. 3:4). Ed Creagan, a Mayo Clinic physician, has done a lot of careful thinking about successful aging. One of the things that he has high on his list of recommendations is that we maintain the ability to laugh well. I think that one of the most important jobs of grandchildren is to make sure their grandparents do a lot of laughing.

I make it a point to laugh with my patients. Some of them are quite sharp and funny: For some reason Betty and I got talking about cats during one of her visits. She was obviously a great cat lover, and I made it clear that cats were not my favorite companions. I had forgotten that little interchange, until her next visit when she rather emphatically announced to me that she had determined to get the best possible medical care. I said, "Oh?" wondering if she had gotten a different doctor or was going to the Mayo Clinic. She proceeded, "Yes, I feel it is only fair to tell you that I have contacted my attorney, and I am willing you my cat!" Fortunately for me, Betty has now outlived her cat.

Being a doctor has given me scores of opportunities to see how a sense of humor helps people cope during times of duress. For example, Rachel, though somewhat demented, was getting on fairly well with the help of her devoted husband. One Sunday night, however, she was admitted to the hospital. When I saw her early on Monday morning, her first comment to me was that she needed to get home. I said, "Well, wait just a minute. Let's see what's going on." "No," she quickly replied, "I want to go home right now. My husband doesn't know where I am, and I want to go now. Come on, I just live over there (pointing nowhere in particular). You're a policeman, and you can get me home." Clearly she was delirious. The next day I saw her on rounds, and after saying good morning I asked if she knew where she was: "Victory Hospital." She got that one right. Then I asked the tough one: "And Rachel, do you know what my name is?" No hesitation now: "Dr. Dunlop." We went through the same routine the next day, only this time when I asked her my name her response was, "If you ask me that one more time, I'm finding a doctor who knows his name!"

I continue to have many good laughs with Betty and Rachel about the cat and the doctor who did not know his name.

Invest in Your Health

Being healthy enables us to continue to function well and serve others. But good health is not to be assumed. Granted, we can't control everything. Some have inherited bad genes that predispose them to a variety of physical ills. But as we age, the state of our health depends less on our genes and more on the choices we make. We must choose to exercise our minds and bodies, maintain a good diet, pursue preventative medical care, and comply with treatment regimens that are helpful. Investing time and energy in maintaining health should be motivated by our love for God. It is one way we can be good stewards of what he has entrusted to us. Appendix 1 includes more discussion of these important subjects.

Avoid the Things That Rob Quality from the Older Years

It is not uncommon for believers to lead vibrant productive lives, but as the years go on some stumble over obstacles that cause them to lose their spiritual vigor. At times this indicates that they have never experienced saving faith and do not have the indwelling Holy Spirit. I suspect more often, though, it is due to their having unrealistic expectations of the end of life. In other cases, the early stages of dementia lead to false mental perceptions.

Some of the things that rob quality include:

Spiritual doubt. The trials and temptations that may cause us to doubt our faith may be more plentiful in our older years than at any other time in our Christian lives. Things may not be going as we had planned or expected. We may cry out to God and feel he does not hear. Nevertheless, we must recognize that we are called to a life of faith. The struggles of aging are a time to press on in faith even as we plead with God to increase our faith.

Discontent. The elderly, like all believers, are to be content. The circumstances that Paul faced were not encouraging, yet he remained content. It has been said that "contentment is a condition of the soul and not of the circumstances."

Worry. Worry not only demonstrates a lack of faith and trust in the Lord, but it may amount to an undue preoccupation with

31

self. If we truly had a passion for the glory of God, rather than our own comfort, we would worry much less.

Loss of the will to keep living well. Recall Fred, whom we talked about earlier. When he sat in the nursing home bed and said, "What's the use?" he was demonstrating a loss of will. I have seen this come for four principle reasons: rationalization, dementia, laziness, and depression.

Rationalization often gives the argument: "I have lived a full life; I'm ready to die. There is no value in my continued living, so Lord take me now." That is how Fred would have expressed it, believing that such thinking made perfect sense. The problem is, the Lord did not take Fred home to heaven when Fred expected, and he kept on living.

It is not infrequent that the personality change of *dementia* may involve a loss of will. It is important for loved ones and caregivers to recognize this cause before they criticize.

Depression is very common in the elderly. It will frequently express itself as tearfulness, preoccupation with death, change in appetite, sleep patterns, etc.

Laziness can be the toughest one to deal with. To some extent Paul addressed this when he wrote: "And we urge you, brothers, admonish the idle, encourage the fainthearted, help the weak, be patient with them all" (1 Thess. 5:14). The idle were the lazy, and they were to be admonished. That was different from the way the weak, who were to be helped, and the fainthearted, who were to be encouraged, were to be treated. The challenge, of course, is determining who is being idle, who is fainthearted, and who is weak. Doing so can take a great deal of spiritual discernment.

I encourage any who are beginning to sense a lack of quality living to review these obstacles and ask if any of these are robbing value from them.

Conclusion

Quality living in our later years involves a series of choices we must make. First we choose to serve others. Then we pursue close friendships and enjoy life together with others. We must be good stewards of our physical and mental health while at the same time carefully avoiding the things that can trip us up. In these ways we accomplish our first strategy to live well till the end.

Prayer
Our Father, how comforting it is to know the value you place on the later days of my life. Help me to steward well the gifts you give me. Lord, I pray that you will give me the faith, strength, and love to continue to work for your kingdom till you call me home. I pray this not for my own comfort but for the glory of your holy name. Amen.

═══════════════ MEDITATION ═══════════════

Fight the good fight with all thy might!
Christ is thy strength, and Christ thy right;
Lay hold on life, and it shall be
Thy joy and crown eternally.

Run the straight race through God's good grace,
Lift up thine eyes, and seek his face;
Life with its way before us lies,
Christ is the path, and Christ the prize.

Cast care aside, lean on thy Guide;
His boundless mercy will provide;
Trust, and thy trusting soul shall prove
Christ is its life, and Christ its love.

"FIGHT THE GOOD FIGHT," JOHN MONSELL (1863)

Let Go Graciously

How do I begin to give up the things of this world?

Does that mean I cannot enjoy God's gifts?

How do this world's values differ from those of heaven?

Is it all right to feel sad about letting go?

How do I maintain hope toward the end of life?

My mother-in-law illustrated much of what I want to say in this chapter. Widowed with three daughters after twenty years of marriage, Mother led a very productive life. She taught junior high school for many years, and after my wife, her youngest, was out of the house, Mother retired and indulged in one of her hobbies, international travel. She sold the family home when she was sixty, downsizing to a two-bedroom condominium. After twenty years she decided to give up that living arrangement for an easier one. She moved to a retirement community where she had her own apartment but had evening meals with friends in the common dining room. Before each of these moves Mother held a garage sale to sell the furniture and other items she could not take to her new, smaller home. In her early eighties, deciding that her eyesight was not good enough for her to drive safely, she sold her car and got around on the bus operated by the association where she lived. Though friends would drive her to church, she never bothered others for her transportation.

By the time she was eighty-five, Mother was declining both physically and mentally. This forced her to depend more on others. My wife drove twelve hours monthly to spend a weekend with her mother. It became clear that Mother needed to make another major life change. We brought her to our place for a week so that we could take her to visit a number of assisted-living facilities. She chose the one we felt would keep her the most active and still be affordable. This move was far from easy for her. It required her to leave St. Louis and the support system that she had built up over eighty-five years and come to a totally new situation. Yet, after an initial adjustment period, she made the transition gracefully. She soon began to give away all of the little "treasures" she had obtained over the years. My sons received her silverware and her good china as well as diamonds from her engagement ring. Mother took great joy in knowing that they would go to their future wives. She then went through her curio cabinet and marked each of her things with the name of someone she knew would enjoy it when she was gone. During the next three years, she endured one mini-medical crisis after another. She had extended stays in several different nursing homes until just before her ninetieth birthday when the Lord called her home. Toward the end Mother had little left of this world's goods. Her great joys were no longer things but the visits of family, reminiscing with friends, and getting outdoors for drives. She especially enjoyed our taking her to a beautiful botanical garden in her wheelchair.

Mother enjoyed many things that belonged to this world and accepted them as evidence of God's goodness to her. She did not find it easy to give them up. Yet she did not cling to them, but successfully let them go with grace and dignity. She embodied strategy 2: Let Go Graciously.

As we age, we will face inevitable losses. After all, much of what we experience in the later years of life is loss. Vernon Grounds, the dean emeritus of Western Seminary in Denver, spoke about the "constrictions of age" on his eighty-seventh birthday. He lumped aging's losses into having less space and less time. Gone were the days of international travel; now his life was confined to a single building. Space was constricted. Time, too, was constricted: no longer could he make long-term plans, since he was conscious that death could come at any time.

Let us not kid ourselves: these losses may be hard to take. For many of us life has been very enjoyable. We can say with the psalmist, "The lines have fallen for me in pleasant places; indeed, I have a beautiful inheritance" (Ps. 16:6). We have had loving relationships, comfortable homes, productive careers, more food than is good for us, along with all of the perks of living in a land of freedom and affluence. God has blessed us, and we never want to discredit or fail to appreciate the gifts that he has richly bestowed on us. Still, we must never confuse the gifts with the Giver. We want to treasure God, not his gifts. Recall what James wrote: "Every good gift and every perfect gift is from above, coming down from the Father of lights with whom there is no variation or shadow due to change" (James 1:17).

The wit and wisdom of C. S. Lewis in the *Screwtape Letters* reminds us that part of the difficulty of giving up on the things of this life is related to sinful desires within us. Senior devil Screwtape advises his apprentice on how to capture the heart of those enjoying the good things of life:

> If, on the other hand, the middle years prove prosperous, our position is even stronger. Prosperity knits a man to the World. He feels that he is "finding his place in it," while really it is finding its place in him. His increasing reputation, his widening circle of acquaintances, his sense of importance, the growing pressure of absorbing and agreeable work, build up in him a sense of being really at home in earth which is just what we want. You will

notice that the young are generally less unwilling to die than the middle-aged and the old.[1]

The question is not will we lose our attachment to this world, but how? Will we be able to let go graciously with appropriate grieving or will we seek to hold onto the things of this life till the bitter end? That is what we want to deal with in this strategy. To organize our thinking about this matter, we will first consider what the Scriptures say about our attitudes to this world. Then I'll explain how we should not only give up the things of the world but also the values. Finally we will turn to the one issue that I have found so perplexing in dealing with believers coming to the end of life: hope.

Biblical Foundation

Scripture speaks frequently about the attitude believers should have toward the things of this life. As is often the case, the Bible presents several perspectives that we must hold in balance.

First, we are to enjoy and be thankful for God's gifts. God delights to shower his children with good things: "Everyone also to whom God has given wealth and possessions and power to enjoy them, and to accept his lot and rejoice in his toil—this is the gift of God" (Eccles. 5:19). God wants us to enjoy the things he has made for us and to give him thanks for them: "For everything created by God is good, and nothing is to be rejected if it is received with thanksgiving" (1 Tim. 4:4). I do not know whether God will take my wife, Dorothy, or me first. Whichever it is, I trust that at the time of death we can be there holding each other, thanking God for the marriage we have had and how he has used our marriage to teach us so much about himself. It is not wrong to treasure the good gifts God has given us.

But, second, we are admonished not to love the world: "Do not love the world or the things in the world. If anyone loves the world, the love of the Father is not in him. For all that is in the world—the desires of the flesh and the desires of the eyes and pride in possessions—is not from the Father but is from the world. And the world is passing away along with its desires, but whoever does the will of God abides forever" (1 John 2:15–17). Note how John qualifies his statement about not loving the world. He refers specifically to the desires of the flesh and the eyes, and the pride in possessions. In other words, he is referring not to God's good creation itself but to desires that belong to the world of sin. This passage does not forbid love and gratitude for the good things God has made. It rules out desires for wrong things, as well as selfish, prideful desires for things otherwise good in themselves. It is possible to make an idol out of even the good gifts God gives us when we misuse them or simply value them more than God himself.

Third, we must make sure that we do not trust God's gifts (our incomes, savings, etc.), but that we put our trust fully in God alone: "As for the rich in this present age, charge them not to be haughty, nor to set their hopes on the uncertainty of riches, but on God, who richly provides us with everything to enjoy" (1 Tim. 6:17). That exhortation not to be haughty is most important, for often our attachment to this world is a result of our own pride.

Let Go of the Things of This World

The motives behind releasing things of this world are often complex. There may be good or bad motives present at the same time. For example, an elderly man may live with his demented wife in their beautiful home as long as possible. In part he is motivated by comfort and the pride he gets from the status of owning a beautiful home and thinking that it is something he has earned and deserved. At the same time he wants to stay in the home because his demented wife is able to function in the familiar surroundings, and, if they sell their home, she will likely need to be institutionalized. The first motives are sinful and represent an over-attachment to this world. The second appear to be purer. As we discuss specific things we must give up, I ask you to recognize the complexity of life and be sensitive to the motives of your heart.

Let Go Gradually and Willingly

Many of the losses associated with aging are inevitable and often forced upon us, but some things we can choose to give up voluntarily. When we can see the losses coming, I have observed that it is much better to recognize them, plan for them, and make changes somewhat gradually and proactively rather than waiting for a crisis to force a drastic change. Doing so keeps more options open. For example, it may be wiser to retire early when you are still able to work part-time at something you enjoy that is more service- than income-driven. You may be able to work at that more relaxed pace for many years longer than if you stayed in your original career. Or perhaps downsizing to a small condo in your seventies may be wiser than living in your long-time home until a crisis incapacitates you and sends you to a nursing home.

Focus on the Positives

Each week my wife meets with a group of dynamic seniors living in an assisted-living facility. They chat and drink tea together, and then Dorothy reads to them. Her assessment of this group is that they choose to focus on what they still have rather than on what they have lost. That attitude makes an immeasurable difference in how they adjust to the losses they frequently face.

Dealing with Specific Losses

Career. Many people do not recognize the difficulties of retiring. Some have had stressful jobs that they have been looking forward to leaving. But there is a danger of focusing more on what you are not going to have to do than on what you will do. Retirement involves a number of losses one needs to face: identity is one of them. Many of us find our identities in our careers. Sometimes people ask me if I feel they are ready to retire. I tend to start with a question (even when I already know the answer): "What do you do?" The answers are usually something like, "I am a chemist," or, "I work for Abbott Labs." If our identities are tied up in what we do, we will say, "I am a ___." When people so closely associate their identities with their careers, retiring can be rough. For some it may be wise to defer retirement. Those who do retire will need to re-create an identity and orient themselves around another role in life: a church leader, a volunteer, a parent, etc. Often, the skills and knowledge that workers used on the job can be employed in other areas, giving them the sense of significance they once had in the workplace.

Besides grappling with the loss of identity, retirees will face loss of status, income, friends, and a sense of accomplishment. There is much to let go of or replace when a person leaves the workplace.

House. Like leaving a job, moving from a home can be tough. Doing so typically involves a number of losses. Earlier we spoke of how choices can be complex and how often they involve mixed motives. To illustrate allow me to share two stories:

First is that of my friend Hans. He has a beautiful home that he and his wife have enjoyed for years. It has become somewhat of a burden for them to maintain, though they receive much help from their son who lives nearby. When Hans and I talked about downsizing, he responded, "John, I know what you are saying, and perhaps I am overly attached to the house, but the thing that gives me the most problems is just the thing that keeps me going the most." I see his point. Hans's home is not a material possession he is unwilling to give up. Rather, its need to be maintained offers him a challenge and a sense of significance.

Second is ninety-year-old, Emma, whose house was a treasured link to the past. She told me how difficult it was to manage the home by herself. I rather blithely said, "Well, then, it's time to give it up." She, too, acknowledged that it might be wrong to be so committed to her house, but, quickly tearing up, she related how she and her husband had built the house themselves in the early years of their marriage. Now that he had been gone for twenty years, she said it was the major thing that still tied her to him. I responded that I could easily recite to her all of the advantages of downsizing and selling her house. However, what she needed to do was to weigh those advantages against the emotional advantages that she had by staying there. I stressed that this was a decision that she would have to make by herself.

Both Hans and Emma could be accused of holding the things of this world too tightly. I do not believe we should be quick to make those judgments.

Our homes can provide a sense of security, especially for the elderly. Undergoing so many losses during the latter years can easily make a move an unnerving experience. All sorts of things wrapped up in a home can make us feel safe: a solid community, reliable neighbors, familiar surroundings, etc. Simply seeing a familiar tree outside the window can give a sense of peace and security.

In recent times, we have become aware of the depth of loss created by a change of residence. For this reason, we may want to help the elderly stay in their familiar homes and communities as long as possible (around-the-clock caregivers and programs such as Meals on Wheels can be helpful). For many, minimizing change and dislocation is best.

While I have mentioned some of the advantages of staying in one's home, there are negatives to consider as well. Living in a private home, particularly in suburbia, is difficult if you can no longer drive or do your own cooking and housework. If help cannot be hired, family, friends, or neighbors must do the chores. Besides eliminating the cost and burden of maintaining a home, moving before you die makes it easier for your family. It can take immense amounts of time to clean out a home that has been lived in for many years and sell it.

But what options are there? Below are some of the pros and cons of different living situations. I am convinced no one situation is right for everyone.

1. Continue to live in the family home. This is what Hans and Emma wanted to do for their unique reasons and is the ideal that many seniors have. But as we observed above, it can be a drain on others. Further, as the ability to get out is more limited, living in the family home is frequently socially isolating.

2. Downsize to an apartment. This option often gives seniors less responsibility and is frequently easier on the family, but it may also be socially isolating. If the apartment is in a senior building, there may be opportunities to build relationships with peers, but not often with younger people. If the complex includes other ages, there is potential for more cross generational interaction, but the younger people may not be interested in engaging in such friendships.

3. Live with children. For many this is the answer. It maximizes contact across generational lines and often allows families to function together the way they should. To use a concept I learned from Dr. Ira Byock, a physician who specializes in end-of-life care, it allows the word *family* to be a verb. I was raised in a home where first my paternal grandfather and later my maternal grandmother lived with us. It gave me a lot of exposure to these grandparents, and I was certainly enriched by them. On the other hand, it was restricting for my parents, as they could never leave home without worrying about and making arrangements for their parents. Those with the means to afford it might build a home with an "in-law apartment" or purchase a duplex to allow the seniors greater independence.

4. Move into assisted living. There are many beautiful facilities developing across the country where seniors can have their own living space, yet have many things provided for them. The residents usually have their own small rooms, a lot of community space, planned activities, nursing care available on site 24/7, and three nutritious meals a day. There are several major drawbacks, however. First, these facilities are expensive; second, they confine social relationships almost exclusively to other seniors; and third, try as they may to be otherwise, they are still to some degree institutional.

5. Move to a nursing home. A nursing home offers the same benefits and the same disadvantages as assisted living, though both to greater degrees. They are most helpful

when they are used as convalescent centers while recovering from a hospitalization. As long-term facilities they may not be so desirable.

In addition to the seniors' social needs, safety should also be considered when choosing where to live. Often the safest situation is not the most appealing. Daniel lived in an assisted-living facility. There he was happy and enjoyed his friends. After a series of falls, his family moved him to a nursing home so that he could be watched more closely. In that respect, it worked; in the three months he was there, he had no falls. Yet, he was miserable, constantly begging to return to where he had been before. He started to withdraw from people, not eat well, and lose weight. Wisely, the family decided that safety was a lesser concern than happiness and allowed him to return to his assisted-living community. He was again happy, engaged in activities, and gained weight. Being involved in community can be very therapeutic.

This issue of safety can often create a conflict of values between seniors and their children. Once, a daughter insisted that it was my job to tell her parents to sell their house and move into an apartment. Knowing how much her mother and father valued their home, I refused to do this. I explained to the daughter that while her highest value was her parents' safety, their highest value was independence. It was not my role to insist that her values take priority over theirs. Needless to say, she was not satisfied with my response.

A key consideration when deciding on a living situation is the impact it may have on the caregiver. Having primary responsibility for the care of a senior can be a most challenging task. It may require a total disruption of the caregiver's family life or career. Though we each have a God-given responsibility to care for aging relatives, that obligation may be fulfilled in a variety of ways, some of which may cause less caregiver stress. We must recall that our commitment to our immediate family or our job can also be based on God's call. There have been multiple studies showing the emotional, physical, and spiritual toll caregiving can bring. The most common cause of depression in women in their fifties is being caregiver for an elderly parent. Clearly the desires, abilities, and other responsibilities of the primary caregiver must be considered carefully in deciding a living situation. The motive may be to honor the parent, but offering substandard care at home because of caregiver fatigue may not be honoring.

Driving. In his book on adult transitions, Charles Sell tells of the time he stood with his father looking at his dad's two-year-old Ford Granada. "Wistfully, he explained that he had been unable to renew his driver's license a few weeks before. Always an active man, he deeply felt the loss of his freedom to move about. Sorrowfully, I stood with him beside his car as I had often stood in a hospital room with others beside the body of their loved one—tearfully sharing his grief with little to say."[2] Giving up driving is very hard. In our culture, the car is often the means of independence, and it may also be the key to one's social connections and attendance at worship services. I do not want to discount these things. In addition, driving and one's living arrangement are related, especially in suburban or rural areas. Sometimes it is not feasible to give up driving until one moves to a living situation where a car is unnecessary. While there are many good reasons for the elderly to want to continue to drive, there are many people who insist on driving long beyond the point of its being practical or safe. Choosing to give up the car and stop driving can be a step toward not being so fiercely independent out of regard for the safety of others.

It is true, however, that even as one loses some cognitive ability, the basic skills of driving are often preserved. I see more problems with seniors getting lost than causing accidents. Many communities have programs provided by the physical therapy departments at rehabilitation centers that offer comprehensive evaluations of driving safety. This type of assessment is much more in-depth than simply passing a state driving test. If a senior is resisting the family's efforts to convince him to give up driving, having an independent evaluation makes sense. The results can either reassure the family of the senior's ability to continue to drive, or else convince the older person that he or she should turn over the keys (with no blame falling to the family).

Possessions. We must learn to give up many of our possessions. Be generous and give them away. You might have heirlooms that you received from your family that you treasure. You are likely in the best position to know who would derive the greatest pleasure from having your things.

Legal Rights. There are times when we can be unduly protective of our legal rights. It is often wise to appoint a power of attorney with financial responsibilities. This is especially true if you develop dementia. My own family came to appreciate the value of that. My father was a godly man who loved to give to the Lord's work. As he grew older, he began to succumb to the constant pressure he received from various political causes. Dad was getting forgetful and clearly had an early dementia. These new political concerns were not the passion of his life. Giving in to the pressures of the politicians, he began writing large checks in response to all of the appeals he received. Fortunately, several years before, he had appointed my sister to be his power of attorney and made her a cosigner on his checking account. She was able to guard him against making choices that were inconsistent with his life's goals. Dad's situation emphasizes the value of designating a power of attorney before dementia sets in, when one is still competent to execute the necessary documents.

As I deal with many of my elderly friends, I am frequently impressed with how difficult letting these things go can be. I look at those who are now in their 90s. They spent their impressionable years during the Depression. They sacrificed to get our nation through World War II. After living through those hardships, they worked hard to raise and provide for their families. It is no wonder that they find it difficult to give things up. Each change brings its own grieving process, for they are losing the things for which they have so often given thanks to God. But with God's help, we can let go of the things of this world with grace and dignity.

Many other things that are out of our control begin to break our attachments to this world. Some of these include:

46

Health. Ecclesiastes 12:1–8 offers an insightful and somewhat humorous commentary on aging.

Fig. 2.1 Aging in Ecclesiastes

Ecclesiastes 12:1–8	Comments
Remember also your Creator in the days of your youth, before the evil days come and the years draw near of which you will say, "I have no pleasure in them"; before the sun and the light and the moon and the stars are darkened and the clouds return after the rain, in the day when the keepers of the house tremble, and the strong men are bent, and the grinders cease because they are few, and those who look through the windows are dimmed, and the doors on the street are shut—when the sound of the grinding is low, and one rises up at the sound of a bird, and all the daughters of song are brought low—they are afraid also of what is high, and terrors are in the way; the almond tree blossoms, the grasshopper drags itself along, and desire fails, because man is going to his eternal home, and the mourners go about the streets—before the silver cord is snapped, or the golden bowl is broken, or the pitcher is shattered at the fountain, or the wheel broken at the cistern, and the dust returns to the earth as it was, and the spirit returns to God who gave it. Vanity of vanities, says the Preacher; all is vanity.	Old age will come Loss of pleasure The whole world looks darker— possibly cataracts Hope is short-lived The body is weaker and stooped Loss of teeth Loss of vision Inability to get out Loss of hearing Early rising/poor sleep Pleasures diminish Multiple fears and phobias Physical dangers in getting out White hair Former leaper now drags Loss of sexual drive Life will end in death All pictures of useful and attractive things that have no more beauty or use Age and death could potentially be the most meaningless aspect of life

Ecclesiastes tells us how to cope with many of the physical losses that may accompany our older years. The key is to "remember your Creator." Remember first that you are a creature and God is the Creator. Several things are implied here. First, God made you with a purpose that is more about him than it is about you. Second, as your Creator he knows everything about you. He knows what makes you tick, and he knows what you need. Third, you can trust that the same care and skill God used when he created you will take you through the losses of the older years. Therefore, Ecclesiastes advises us to remember our Creator, which will equip us to go through the losses of our later years well. How simple yet how profound is that advice!

Mental sharpness. Many of us identify our self-worth with our IQs. That is far from the biblical teaching that grounds our value in the fact that we are made in God's image and redeemed by Christ. Nevertheless, we easily lapse into thinking that our worth is tied to our intelligence, and the sharper we have been over the years, the more likely we are to take pride in our intellects. Losing our mental sharpness may be one of God's ways of helping us to loosen our grasp on this life.

Financial security. You retired thirty years ago with a very conservative financial plan. You made the best projections you could based on estimates of a 2 percent return on your investments. The problem is that you did not plan on the stock market's losing 25 percent of your net worth in several months, and you did not plan to be alive at ninety-five. Now you are running out of funds at the same time as your expenses are increasing. Trusting God may be a challenge.

Friends and loved ones. Saying good-bye to friends and loved ones helps us hold this world more loosely. It seems the older we get, the more funerals we attend. Many of my older friends are the only survivors of their families. Widows and widowers have already had to say good-bye to the one they had shared their lives with. Vigen Guroian has wisely written, "Death would not be so bitter were it not that love makes life so sweet. Nor would death inspire such fear and dread were it not that it cuts us off from those whom we love and who love us."[3] Let there be no question, this is one of the most difficult issues of all. It is hard for the dying to leave those they love and equally hard for the survivors to let go of the dying. This is not because of a sinful attachment to this world; this is rejoicing in the gracious gifts of God. Yet this may be another way that God prepares us to die.

Although there may be some beneficial results from giving up our attachments to this world, we must never belittle how difficult it is. We will see in strategy 5 that death is a part of the curse. It is because of these losses that it is appropriate for us to lament and cry out against death.

Dealing with Grief

The major reaction to the losses we face as we approach our final years is grief. Though people grieve differently and do not handle losses in the same way, research reveals that most share a similar experience. Understanding this process can help us as we go through it. To be sure, loss is terrible. Grief is painful. It smears our thinking with sorrow and sometimes provokes anger and resentment.

Yet, grieving is fertile soil in which character may grow. The losses may leave scars, but they can create character and spiritual growth. "Suffering produces endurance, and endurance produces character, and character produces hope" (Rom. 5:3–4).

Maturing demands that everyone learn how to handle grief, simply because all of us will lose or give up something we cherish someday. Death is only one means of deprivation. A geographic move finds people mourning a whole community and a host of friends left behind. Adults of all ages lose jobs, billfolds, friends, and loved ones. In old age, grieving can be more complicated when one loss compounds another. Further, the older we are the less hopeful we may be that sustaining a loss will quickly lead to a fresh start.

Grief is neither abnormal nor wrong for the Christian. The apostle Paul admitted that if his friend Epaphroditus were to die, Paul would suffer intense grief (Phil. 2:25–27). After the martyr Stephen was killed, "devout men . . . made great lamentation over him" (Acts 8:2). In ancient times people were not ashamed to display grief.

Accepting the legitimacy of grief will help us prepare for it. The one who believes he should not experience sorrow or "break down" may have a difficult time with loss. Grief is not an enemy to be attacked with Scripture verses about joy or with sweet-sounding phrases. It is not something to escape; it is a tunnel to go through, not fly over. We must name and talk about our losses and then accept them rather than denying the feelings we have. God's Word and presence can enable us to come out the other end of the tunnel stronger and more firm in our faith. It's best not to try to stop people from grieving when they have cause to. When someone we know must move to a nursing home or surrender her driver's license, we may simply have to stand by and allow her to process these losses for herself. Like stirring a stagnant pool of water, loss brings all sorts of emotions to the surface.

Obviously, the primary reaction to grief is sadness. But grievers should be aware that they might also need to deal with the troubling emotions of anger, resentment, guilt, and bitterness that sometimes occur. These can damage relationships with others as well as cause disturbing mental anguish. Some of these emotions may be surprising, such as fear. A grieving C. S. Lewis was blindsided by the feeling: "No one ever told me that grief felt so like fear. I am not afraid, but the sensation is like being afraid. The same fluttering in the stomach, the same restlessness, the yawning. I keep on swallowing."[4] Though Lewis writes that he was not afraid, often grief can actually produce real fear: fear of the future, of being able to cope, of death. That kind of fear is rarely based on truth, is not of God, and can be destructive to the spirit. Sudden loss makes a person feel vulnerable, wondering, "If this could happen, what could be next?"

Also, we should recognize how our emotions can affect our thinking. We should try not to take seriously all the thoughts that our feelings generate. In grief, C. S. Lewis can be excused for pondering God as some sort of monster who loves to torture people. Later in *A Grief Observed*, he explains that his mental pictures were painted by emotional brush strokes. "Why do I make room in my mind for such filth and nonsense? Do I hope that if feeling disguises itself as thought I shall feel less? Aren't all these notes the senseless writhings of a man who won't accept the fact that there is nothing we can do with suffering except to suffer it?"[5]

Despite all the disturbing features of grief, it is still possible to speak seriously of "good grief." In the end, the griever comes to acceptance. He or she is ready to move on and live with the memory of the loss, but not its pain.

Let the Values of This World Go

It is not only the things of this world that we must let go but many of its values as well. Too often, false values have crept into our own thinking. We must divest ourselves of these before we are prepared to enter God's holy presence.

Self-Esteem

This is a worldly value if there ever were one. Yet, how much do I buy into it myself? Often my self-esteem is based upon my intellect, appearance, or accomplishments and not on the fact that I am made in God's image and redeemed by Christ. I am proud of my career as a doctor. I love to get on the track at the health club and run circles around those who are younger. I love the applause that comes at the end of a class I have taught. But deep within my heart I know it is all a charade. It is only by the grace of God I am what I am. Sure, I may have made some good choices, but it is only because he put me in a situation where I could make them and gave me the motivation to choose what was right. Still, I will not always be able to make the correct diagnosis, I will not always be able to do the ten-mile run, and I will not always be healthy. I will eventually recognize deep within my soul that I can only boast in what God has done. I will eventually agree with the prophet Jeremiah who, more than 2,500 years ago, wrote: "Let not the wise man boast in his wisdom, let not the mighty man boast in his might, let not the rich man boast in his riches, but let him who boasts boast in this, that he understands and knows me, that I am the LORD who practices steadfast love, justice, and righteousness in the earth. For in these things I delight, declares the LORD" (Jer. 9:23–24). This loss of self-esteem is good. It gives the glory not to us but to the Lord who deserves it, and it is a significant part of weaning our hearts away from this world to be prepared for our eternal home.

Self-Sufficiency

Self-sufficiency is very close to self-esteem and is often one of the sources of it. I like to refer to the *ministry of dependence*, how we help others by not being too fiercely independent. Many times we need the humility that allows others to serve us. Over the years we have been too quick to respond to offers of help with, "No thanks, I can do it myself."

Yet, giving others the opportunity to serve us can bless both the served and the server. Recall these lines from Shakespeare:

> The quality of mercy is not strain'd
> It droppeth as the gentle rain from heaven
> Upon the place beneath; it is twice bless'd;
> It blesseth him that gives and him that takes.[6]

My father was a great dad. He was a successful businessman, and he was committed to the Lord. But he was very independent and quite used to doing things his way. One afternoon when Dorothy and I were visiting my parents in their apartment during Dad's final weeks on earth, he asked me to help him use the toilet. I rolled his wheelchair into the bathroom and helped him sit on his raised toilet seat. I went to leave, but he motioned for me to stay. He did his business, tore off some toilet paper, and looked at me questioningly. In his weakness he handed me the toilet paper, nodding his head affirmatively. I took the paper and cleaned him off, pulled his pants up, transferred him to the wheelchair, and took him back to the others without his saying a word. I realized that five decades earlier, Dad probably did the same for me, and now we had come full circle. My relationship with my father took on an entirely new meaning as he allowed me to serve him in that very personal way. Ira Byock speaks of how when the dying give their loved ones the privilege to serve, they are helping the loved ones to complete the relationship and also aiding in their future grieving process. I have found that to be true.

There is an essential humility that makes us willing to be served. Christians should have learned at the time of their salvation that they can do nothing to save themselves but are totally dependent on God. Throughout life a desire for self-sufficiency can impair spiritual growth. At the end of life, it is good to be less self-sufficient and trust God more fully.

What about Hope?

Over and over again I have found that the most difficult thing to give up when we are critically or even terminally ill is a hope for a cure and continued life on earth. I frequently struggle with that myself; most doctors and other medical people do as well. It is frequently only at the very end that we can relinquish this hope. On the other hand, I am fully aware that it is our desire to cling to hope that so often prevents us from preparing for death as we should and may prompt unduly aggressive medical care.

My good friend Dr. George Sweeting, retired president of Moody Bible Institute, has said that we can live forty days without food, three days without water, three minutes without air, and three seconds without hope. We know that hope is a Christian virtue. We must never discredit its value. Paul wrote, "May the God of hope fill you with all joy and peace in believing, so that by the power of the Holy Spirit you may abound in hope" (Rom. 15:13).

Forty-five-year-old Lynn had been seriously ill since her teenage years with recurrent life-threatening infections. She had developed a severe disabling arthritis and had required multiple surgeries on her joints. She also had a clotting disorder and cycled between life-threatening hemorrhages and life-threatening blood clots. In the last years of her life, it seemed as if she was in the hospital more than she was at home. The amazing thing about

Lynn was how she cared so much about others and accepted her own problems with equanimity. Everyone loved her. About three months before her eventual death, I told her how much I respected her desire to fight for life, but that we needed to recognize that if she continued to deteriorate as much in the months ahead as she had in the months gone by, she would not live more than six months. I suggested she let me know what she felt about end-of-life care, and I suggested she fill out an advance directive. Her response was, "No! You're not giving up hope, are you?" Lynn died in the intensive care unit after repeated failed attempts at resuscitation. She had never talked to her family about death, and they had no plans when she died. She was steadfast in her hope in this life.

A good friend of mine has another close friend dying of cancer. I suggested they have a talk about when it would be appropriate to forgo aggressive life-sustaining treatment. My friend was hesitant to do this lest he imply that his friend give up hope.

Audrey is ninety-nine years old. She is successfully living in an assisted-living facility, but she is deteriorating, and all signs indicate that she might have colon cancer. Together with her guardian we have decided not to do any tests, because with all of her other medical problems, she would not be a candidate for surgery or for other treatments. I have also suggested that as she gets weaker, we may need to move her to a nursing home. Her guardian has been emphatic: no way am I to tell Audrey that she may have cancer and no way should she be moved to the nursing home. Why? The guardian simply states, "Audrey would give up and lose all hope."[7]

As you can see, hope is a daily challenge. We need hope, and we should never give it up. The question must be asked, though, "What are we to hope in?" I present and critique three possible answers to this question:

1. Hope for a cure and continued life on earth. Hope in this life is good. It is well known that the medical pro-fession is frequently in error when it comes to medical

prognoses. Studies show that more commonly, doctors overestimate the time left to live, but not infrequently it goes the other way, too. Breakthroughs in medicine are made all the time, and there is reason to hope in science. But it is not just medicine that allows us to hope for a cure. Scripture commands us to pray: "Is anyone among you sick? Let him call for the elders of the church, and let them pray over him, anointing him with oil in the name of the Lord" (James 5:14). God will at times heal in response to our prayers. When we pray, we are not to do it with a sense of entitlement or of telling God what to do. Rather, we come as little children letting our requests be made known to God.[8] Nevertheless, whether hope is founded in God, in medicine, or in both, it can be taken too far. When we offer hope for cure and longer life, we should always do so in the spirit of "hope for the best, prepare for the worst." If we do not do this, then hope will stand in the way of successfully bringing our lives to closure. Ultimately, we must be aware that hope for a long life will be doomed to failure. As Paul wrote, "If in this life only we have hoped in Christ, we are of all people most to be pitied" (1 Cor. 15:19).

2. Hope in heaven. Christians enjoy the hope of eternal life with God. This hope in heaven is a vital part of ending life well. It is intriguing, however, that some people have so little reason for their optimism. I recall John, who was dying of cancer. I asked him if he had a hope in heaven. He smiled and said, "I sure do." I asked what he was basing his hope on. His response was that while serving in Vietnam, he was almost killed by a rocket. As he lay on the ground dazed and thinking that he was dying, everything around him appeared to be bright. He took that to mean that he was going to heaven, so he had no concerns. So many others are convinced that they are going to heaven because they have not been as bad as other people. They hope that their good life will earn them a place in God's

heaven. Unfortunately, that is not what the Scriptures teach. They clearly teach that our hope must be placed in God and in his grace given to us through Christ.

Hope in heaven is something all true believers in Christ should have. When the Bible uses hope in this context, it is not a hope against the odds but rather a firm and sure expectation: "We have this as a sure and steadfast anchor of the soul, a hope . . ." (Heb. 6:19).

But eternal hope, too, can be used inappropriately. Louise had spent fifty years as a missionary, taking the gospel to remote villages. She was a trooper. Yet she had a bad heart and at seventy-five had to retire to this country. She continued to be active in the Lord's service, but this too was short-lived. So Louise decided that it was her time to die, and she would simply go to bed till the Lord took her home. I tried to tell her that her decision was premature. I told her about when I first went to summer camp at age seven. Camp was the third week of July, but I had my bag packed and was ready to go by the middle of June. I was miserable for the next month. I told Louise that she had packed her bag too early, but she would not listen. She had an awesome hope in heaven, but it did not prepare her to use the life the Lord had given her on earth. She died two years after giving up.

3. Hope in God. This is the believer's most appropriate hope. We trust that God will do what is right. The question is never whether he wants us to live. The fundamental question is, do we believe that he is good and that he is in control of the situation, allowing us to have hope in him? The Psalms repeatedly exhort us to "hope in God." Remember Lynn? She was unwilling to give up hope. Had her hope been in God, she never would have had to give that up.

Conclusion

God has richly blessed many of us in this life. We have enjoyed his gifts for many years. Yet, there inevitably comes a time when we must say good-bye to the things of this world, a time when we come to embrace the things and values of eternity. Letting go is perhaps what we hate most about death. Loosening our ties to this world is rarely an easy process, but I find it is essential in order to come to the end of life well. An important part of this process is realigning our hope. We do not want to give up hope, but we must learn that rather than hoping for a long healthy life, we must begin to find our only hope in the Lord—that he is good and that he will do what is right.

Prayer

Lord Jesus, I thank you for giving me such a rich life. You have blessed me with so many things: family, health, independence, and possessions. I never want to confuse your gifts with yourself. Help me to hold these gifts loosely to free my heart to love you more.

MEDITATION

Take the world, but give me Jesus,
Sweetest comfort of my soul;
With my Savior watching o'er me,
I can sing though billows roll.

Take the world, but give me Jesus,
Let me view his constant smile;
Then throughout my pilgrim journey
Light will cheer me all the while.

Take the world, but give me Jesus,
All its joys are but a name;
But his love abideth ever,
Through eternal years the same.

57

Take the world, but give me Jesus.
In his cross my trust shall be,
Till, with clearer, brighter vision,
Face to face my Lord I see.

Refrain
Oh, the height and depth of mercy!
Oh, the length and breadth of love!
Oh, the fullness of redemption,
Pledge of endless life above!

"TAKE THE WORLD,
BUT GIVE ME JESUS,"
FANNY CROSBY (1879)

Treasure God's Love; Love Him in Return

What is it like to truly experience God's love?

How should I respond to God's love?

How does knowing God's love impact my view of death?

What will it be like to never again experience evil?

How should the church equip us to finish life well?

Ken was diagnosed with terminal cancer of the pancreas while in his early forties. As a teenager he had come into a personal relationship with God by trusting Jesus. He saw how much God loved him by reflecting on Jesus' death on the cross. He responded with a deep, passionate love for God, and attempted to serve him faithfully. He accepted his diagnosis with a calm assurance that God was in control. Ken lived for six months after learning of his illness and was an inspiration to many. Up until a month before he died, he was out speaking to church and civic groups, always telling of the love of God and the hope that gave him of eternal life. Ken longed to be in the presence of this God who loved him so much. When he died, it was as if he peacefully responded to a call from God. From an earthly perspective, dying that young was tragic, but from the perspective of eternity, it was victorious. Ken lived out so well what I consider to be the most important strategy to finish life well: strategy 3: Treasure God's Love; Love Him in Return.

Treasure God's Love

Many of us were taught about God's love as children. We sang, "Jesus loves me, this I know, for the Bible tells me so." But did we really grasp the enormity of God's love? Paul knew just how important it was for us to take hold of this powerful truth. He prayed this for the Ephesians:

> So that Christ may dwell in your hearts through faith—that you, being rooted and grounded in love, may have strength to comprehend with all the saints what is the breadth and length and height and depth, and to know the love of Christ that surpasses knowledge, that you may be filled with all the fullness of God. (Eph. 3:17–19)

Paul is not talking about something that simply occurs in our brains. No, he speaks of the *heart*. In the New Testament the heart was the focus of mind, feeling, and will; it stood for the whole personality.[1] Paul sees that the end result of our experience of the love of Christ will be that we are filled with the fullness of God himself. Nineteenth-century evangelist D. L. Moody illustrates the intensity of this type of experience: "Well, one day, in the city of New York—oh, what a day!—I cannot describe it, I seldom refer to it; it is almost too sacred an experience to name. . . . I can only say that God revealed Himself to me, and I had such an experience of His love that I had to ask Him to stay His hand."[2] It is this type of experience that Paul wanted the Ephesians to have. I am grateful that there have been times in my life when I have experienced God's love, though not to the intensity Moody described. They have not been frequent or long-lasting, but they have been unforgettable and foundational to my understanding of God. I have known many Christians who understand God's love in their minds, but they have never experienced his love in their inner beings. Paul prayed that they would. We must first have an intellectual understanding of the love of God, and then we must earnestly pray that the Holy Spirit will allow us to have a deep, fulfilling experience of his love. It is that sequence of first knowing and then experiencing, that will allow us to treasure God's love.[3]

To understand God's love, we must start with basic theology. Scripture teaches that in the beginning God was. There was nothing that was not God. He presented himself to Moses as "I AM WHO I AM" (Ex. 3:14). Theologians would say that God alone is self-existent. Only God exists simply because he exists. He is primary; everything else was created and is thereby secondary. What that means is that everything is fundamentally about him. Rick Warren got it right when he opened his book *The Purpose-Driven Life* by telling us, "It's not about you."[4]

This God-centered view of the world is consistent with what the apostle Paul taught so forcefully: "For from him and through him and to him are all things. To him be glory forever. Amen" (Rom. 11:36). Paul knew that God was the source of all things; they are "from him." Furthermore, he knew that God was the means to accomplish anything of eternal value; all things are "through him." Finally, God is the purpose or goal of all things; they are "to him." Paul then affirms that the ultimate purpose of all creation is that God is glorified. This must become the passion and purpose of our lives. We were created to demonstrate God's glory, and that is the only way we will find comfort and fulfillment. It is fitting that Paul closes this doxology with "Amen"—so be it, there is nothing more to be said.

From the beginning God was a defined entity. It is as if he were enclosed in a circle. That circle included everything that was God. We can think of that circle as his holiness. Holiness means to be set apart. God created a world for his glory. Genesis says of each step of creation that "It was good." Everything God made (plants, animals, etc.) was within the circle of his holiness, completely consistent with his character, the only possible standard for what could be called "good." Included in that good creation were such things as life, righteousness, love, peace, health, renewable ecology, etc.

Human life as well was created for God's glory. Isaiah put it succinctly: ". . . everyone who is called by my name, whom I created for my glory, whom I formed and made" (Isa. 43:7). Adam and Eve, while enjoying God's presence in the garden, experienced a fulfillment that is beyond what we can comprehend. They found their joy in God, and God was glorified as they found pleasure in him. God loved them, and they loved God in return.

But their joy in God was disrupted when they disobeyed God and in so doing stepped out of the circle of God's holiness. I am not sure that any of us understand the cataclysmic results of their sin. No longer was the world "good" as God created it. No longer did all things work together perfectly. In fact the whole system began to unravel. Now there was sin, disease, death, hate, and war, and ecology was no longer renewable. All this a consequence of what theologians call the "fall." Humanity is outside of the circle of God's holiness.

But, thankfully, there is good news. God's loving nature was not satisfied that his creation should remain apart from him. God provided a remedy. Perhaps the best-known verse in the Bible is John 3:16: "For God so loved the world, that he gave his only Son, that whoever believes in him should not perish but have eternal life." God sent his Son to make it possible for us, his disobedient creatures, to reenter the circle of God's holiness. Paul says, "but God shows his love for us in that while we were still sinners, Christ died for us" (Rom. 5:8) and, "but God, being rich in mercy, because of the great love with which he loved us, even when we were dead in our trespasses, made us alive together with Christ—by grace you have been saved" (Eph. 2:4–5). God did not take such a drastic step to allow us to reenter his circle of holiness because we deserved it or because he needed to have us; he gave his Son simply to display God's own goodness and glory. Now, as a result of the death of Jesus, death can become life; hate can become love; and sin can become righteousness. It is in Jesus' coming to earth and his death on the cross that we are able to see how much God loves us.

With the death of Jesus serving as the foundation for our understanding of God's love, we learn two important lessons: First, God's love as evidenced in the death of Christ assures us that God will continue to provide for our needs: "He who did not spare his own Son but gave him up for us all, how will he not also with him graciously give us all things?" (Rom. 8:32).

Second, God's love is not something that we earn but is a gift that he freely gives to us. That is the meaning of God's grace: "For by grace you have been saved through faith. And this is not your own doing; it is the gift of God, not a result of works, so that no one may boast" (Eph. 2:8–9). I truly believe this, yet I find myself constantly lapsing into a pattern of thinking that would contradict it. Instead of rejoicing in God's love and enjoying him, I continuously revert to thinking that either I must be good enough to earn God's love or that I never really was all that bad and deserved it after all. Then I start thinking that since God loved me, I must have been lovable, and instead of exalting him, I find I am exalting myself. No! God's love is truly by grace; it is not earned.

We should seek to sense the love of God for each of us as individuals in far deeper ways. First understand his love for you in your mind, but then allow yourself to sit back, relax, and feel the intensity of his embrace, allowing yourself not only to know but to experience his love for you in your inner being. Treasure God's love, and it will equip you to come to the end of life well.

Love Him in Return
Treasuring God's love for us enables us to be lovers ourselves: "We love because he first loved us" (1 John 4:19). Jesus spoke of the two greatest commandments: "You shall love the Lord your

God with all your heart and with all your soul and with all your strength and with all your mind, and your neighbor as yourself" (Luke 10:27). There are times when I have looked on these commands as rather onerous, believing that to follow them requires a life of harsh, doleful sacrifice. But then I pause and think for a minute. Jesus requires not that we *do* something (which would be work), but that we *love* someone. Who really can object to being in love? Love is not a burden. True love allows that any activity done for the other, even if it is sacrificial, is joyful. Besides, we are not only called to love a person, but to love the Supreme Being in the universe. He created us to love him and offers us what we most need—himself. On a human level, whenever I am deeply conscious of the love my wife has for me, it is never a burden to love her in return. My emotions automatically respond to her love for me. How much more natural and thrilling it should be to respond to the love of the heavenly Father! That is the point of the Bible's metaphor of Jesus being the bridegroom and the church being the bride. The bridegroom is the great lover who woos his bride. She then naturally and with great joy responds lovingly to him.

Our love for God should lead us to the greatest joy in this life even though in a physical sense we are absent from him. The apostle Peter knew that well: "Though you have not seen him, you love him. Though you do not now see him, you believe in him and rejoice with joy that is inexpressible and filled with glory" (1 Pet. 1:8).

Furthermore, our love for God should both define and enrich our own character. John Piper, in his book *Desiring God*, popularized this insightful quote from Henry Scougal: "The worth and excellency of a soul is to be measured by the object of its love."[5]

Longing for God's Presence

A natural outcome of our loving God will be a desire to be in his presence. We will seek experiences in our daily lives when we can savor communion with him. But even apart from this life, the future he promises us is beyond description, as the apostle Paul wrote: "What no eye has seen, nor ear heard, nor the heart of man imagined, what God has prepared for those who love him" (1 Cor. 2:9). We will look forward to the day when we will be in his presence throughout all of eternity. The Psalms speak well to this desire to be in God's presence both now and for eternity:

> You make known to me the path of life;
>   in your presence there is fullness of joy;
>   at your right hand are pleasures forevermore. (Ps. 16:11)

> O God, you are my God; earnestly I seek you;
>   my soul thirsts for you;
> my flesh faints for you,
>   as in a dry and weary land where there is no water.
> So I have looked upon you in the sanctuary,
>   beholding your power and glory.
> Because your steadfast love is better than life,
>   my lips will praise you. (Ps. 63:1–3)

Too often we underestimate our capacity for joy and pleasure. We are tempted to find fulfillment in the sinful things of this life and in our puny selves. When we pursue pleasures in lesser things, we forfeit the opportunity to find our greatest fulfillment in the greatness of God, and we will never ultimately be satisfied. God says it is like drinking water from mud-filled holes in the ground when we could have it from a deeply refreshing stream. That is what Jeremiah referenced when he wrote:

> For my people have committed two evils:
> they have forsaken me,
>   the fountain of living waters,
> and hewed out cisterns for themselves,
>   broken cisterns that can hold no water. (Jer. 2:13)

My own father had followed the Lord from age nineteen. He died in his eighty-fourth year. Near the end, Dad had cancer and was increasingly demented. I well remember sitting with him on what proved to be his last Sunday on earth, listening on the radio to Dr. Erwin Lutzer preaching at Moody Church. Lutzer's subject was the judgment seat of Christ. Dad had never been a very expressive individual, and I never recall him giving a thumbs-up gesture in his entire life. But three times in the message, as Pastor Lutzer referred to standing in the Lord's presence, Dad came out of his quiet reverie, smiled, and put his thumb up. He knew where he was going, and he was longing for the presence of God. That one experience allowed me to feel a great sense of peace with his dying.

One of the spiritual giants I had the honor of being exposed to in my youth was Dr. V. Raymond Edman, then chancellor of Wheaton College. On September 22, 1967, he spoke to the entire college community on what it was like to be invited into the presence of a king. In the middle of his message, Dr. Edman collapsed with a massive heart attack and was taken into the Lord's presence. He was invited into the presence of the Great King whom he loved.

Just as I saw with Dr. Edman and my dad, I have observed that many of my believing patients who have a passionate love for God and longing for his presence are the ones who can most easily slip into his heavenly presence when God calls them home.

Longing for Godliness

Another natural outcome of our understanding God's love and loving him in return is that we will increasingly be distressed by sin not only in our own lives but also in the world around us. Daily we wrestle with temptation. Why can't we keep our minds and motives pure? Why are we so taken up with ourselves and our accomplishments? Why is there so much evil in the world? We pray, "Thy kingdom come, thy will be done, on earth as it is in heaven." We long to be back in the circle of God's holiness. But we are not there yet. Christ died, was buried, and has been raised from the dead. God has given us saving faith, but our salvation is not yet complete. We only have the promise that redemption will someday be completed. In the meantime, we live between the provision of the remedy for our sin and its final fulfillment.

We look forward to an eternity where we will be free from sin and tempted to sin no more. The apostle John wrote: "No longer will there be anything accursed, but the throne of God and of the Lamb will be in it, and his servants will worship him" (Rev. 22:3). In heaven none of the results of sin's curse will exist, save for the scars on the body of Jesus.

Longing for Our Resurrected Body

While living on earth, it is not uncommon that the limitations of our physical bodies interfere with our being able to experience God's love to the fullest. We long for glorified bodies that will far exceed our present bodies in their ability to enjoy God. I doubt that many truly understand the consequences of sin on our bodies. Similarly, many of us have little inkling of what the promised eternal resurrected body will be like. We do know that "he will wipe away every tear from their eyes, and death shall be no more, neither shall there be mourning, nor crying, nor pain anymore, for the former things have passed away" (Rev. 21:4). No longer will the weakness, forgetfulness, or pains of aging distract us from experiencing the fullness of God. In heaven we will be back in the circle of God's holiness. We will have bodies that are the way God intended them to be.

The Role of the Church

The church must play a key role in helping believers through the later years of life. Its most important task is to provide an eternal perspective on the changes of aging. Christians need to be reminded that God loves them and that he is able to meet their needs. They need to see the challenges they face in light of the death and resurrection of Jesus. They need to be continually reminded of the hope that they have in heaven. Through praise, the preaching of the Word, corporate prayer, and words of encouragement from fellow believers, the transitions of aging will become less onerous.

But the church must provide more than spiritual help. Given the many physical and emotional needs of seniors as well as caregivers, the church can do much to help. The challenge is that the needs are great and often require long-term commitments. An all-church workday twice a year will not provide sufficient help. Scripture makes it clear that the church has the responsibility to care for needy seniors. These were primarily widows without families, who were in need. Some seniors need financial help, others need assistance with household chores or transportation, and many desire companionship and friendship. Caregivers need some respite to allow them to get out and have time for other things, including their own peace of mind. The church can provide many of these services, and by doing so can allow the recipients to experience the love of God in very tangible ways.

Conclusion

God loves us to an extent that goes far beyond our ability to comprehend. He created us for his glory. He made Adam and Eve perfect to be compatible with the world he made. Genesis says all of God's creation was "good." It was all-consistent with his holiness. In Adam, we stepped out of this circle of holiness at the fall. God invites us to come back into the circle, having sent his Son to die for us to restore our fellowship with him. That is what our life on earth is all about. And as Christians, we have the hope of an eternity in God's presence, freed from the sin and physical limitations we experience on earth.

To summarize what the last two strategies are about, I would say: To the extent that we can understand and experience God's love for us, develop a longing for God, and find ourselves increasingly satisfied with him more than all other things in this life, we will be prepared to die and to enter his presence. We will find what we have longed for and more. But, if we are grasping onto the things of this earth, we will never be fulfilled.

Prayer

Father, I know that you are the fountain of life, the source of all joy. I long to know you better. I long to be in your presence and to enjoy you forever. In this world I groan. I groan because of the destruction that sin brings in me and in the world around me. I groan as my body is sick and weak. It is just getting worse. I know that you have prepared a better place for me. I look forward to the day when I can be with you eternally, free from sin and having a body that is capable of experiencing your glory to a far greater extent than I can now. May my experience of your love and my love for you spur me on to live well till you call me home.

MEDITATION

Jesus, the very thought of thee
with sweetness fills the breast;
but sweeter far thy face to see,
and in thy presence rest.

O hope of every contrite heart,
O joy of all the meek,
to those who fall, how kind thou art!
How good to those who seek!

But what to those who find? Ah, this
nor tongue nor pen can show;
the love of Jesus, what it is,
none but his loved ones know.

Jesus, our only joy be thou,
as thou our prize wilt be;
Jesus, be thou our glory now,
and through eternity.

"JESUS, THE VERY THOUGHT OF THEE,"
BERNARD OF CLAIRVEAUX
(TWELFTH CENTURY)

Grow through Adversity

Is it possible for suffering to accomplish something good?

What can we learn from Job?

How does our understanding of God impact our response to suffering?

Does God have purpose in our suffering?

How should we respond when we hurt?

Several years ago I was seeing patients the day after I had run a marathon. One patient, an elderly man, greeted me with, "I understand you ran the marathon yesterday." I smiled and agreed. He continued, seemingly impressed, "That's twenty-six miles isn't it?" Knowing that he could take some ribbing, I responded, "No sir, it's twenty-six point two miles. Don't forget the point two; it was the toughest two-tenths of a mile I ever ran." So it is, too, for many who know the end of their life is near. Our later days may be the most difficult. The apostle Paul put it this way:

"Through many tribulations we must enter the kingdom of God" (Acts 14:22).

How are we to deal with the challenges of the end of life? As we endure pain and suffering, will we still say that God is good? Will these difficulties weaken or strengthen our faith? Suffering has the potential to drive us from God. The question, "Why would a good God permit bad things to happen?" has no doubt created a lot of disbelief. I've even known believers who have permitted adversity to drive them from God. Some want little to do with a god who allows them to suffer.

Advice for handling hardships is plentiful, found in whole books or simple slogans such as, "When life hands you a lemon, make lemonade." As a physician who regularly sees people endure multiple losses, I have thought a lot about what to say to them. I know for certain that quips about lemons and lemonade won't be enough to keep them from despairing or feeling their disappointment in God. No, we should never give trite responses to others, especially when they are experiencing great difficulties. I do not believe we should teach difficult concepts (such as those we will review later in this chapter) to those in the midst of much suffering, either. When someone is suffering, it is often best to offer our presence and our compassion, along with our tears.

The Bible offers many insights that help us to endure difficulties well—insights that are far from being trite. The key is that we must study and understand these truths before it is our turn to suffer. The church should be preparing the saints to suffer well. There *is* a Christian way to avoid being defeated by end-of-life adversities, as distressing as they might be. I describe it in strategy 4: Grow through Adversity.

Though it may be a radical idea, the Bible tells us that instead of separating us from God, suffering has the potential to bring us nearer to him. I call that "suffering productively." The Anglican Book of Common Prayer includes the following request: "Sanctify, O Lord, the sickness of your servant *(name),* that the sense of his weakness may add strength to his faith and seriousness to his repentance; and grant that he may live with you in everlasting life; through Jesus Christ Our Lord. *Amen.*" We must recognize the Lord's presence when we suffer and learn to lean more on him.

Suffering in the Bible

To understand suffering and therefore to be able to endure it well, we must consider what the Bible has to say about the downers of life.

Job

That good can grow out of our suffering is the central truth of the book of Job. This idea is not couched in the form of an argument, a sermon, or a glib slogan, but is packaged as a story. The book of Job describes the vital throbbing of a human spirit exploring his inner hopes, doubts, convictions, and trembling emotional upheavals. Far from a frivolous dismissal of the pangs of suffering, the book is a realistic description of the intense agony and struggle Job endured. Yet it shows how one can work through suffering to experience a deeper and more satisfying relationship with God.

The plot of Job is well known. The main character, Job, is introduced as a richly blessed man of the East who is faultlessly faithful to God. Satan comes before God and claims that Job is loyal to God only because God has done great things for him. To test Job, God allows Satan to attack him on all fronts: he takes away Job's wealth, his children, his health, and the compassion of his wife.

While Job's story teaches us it is possible to ultimately accept extreme adversity, it also makes clear that getting to that point may not be easy. Perhaps, through Job's experience, God is teaching us that it is okay to wrestle with questions about our situation even as we endure emotional turmoil. When Job was in so much pain, he cursed the day he was born: "Why did I not die at birth . . . ?" (Job 3:11). At times he was depressed and disheartened: "I am not at ease, nor am I quiet; I have no rest, but trouble comes" (Job 3:26). Agonizing over what is happening, he thinks he is

73

experiencing the brunt of God's wrath: "For the arrows of the Almighty are in me; my spirit drinks their poison; the terrors of God are arrayed against me" (Job 6:4).

Yet Job remains faithful. He cannot, however, accept that his suffering is a punishment for sin. He cries out for God to come to him with an explanation. Job believes God is far greater than he can ever imagine and fully trusts God's essential goodness. Job acknowledges that God is beyond his ability to comprehend: "How small a whisper do we hear of him! But the thunder of his power who can understand?" (Job 26:14). Throughout the book, Job never questions that God is ultimately responsible for all of his calamities. Job has a concept of God that is big enough to enable him to suffer productively.

His friends, however, have a different view of God. They feel they know and understand God. They defend his goodness and say that he would not afflict anyone without reason. They, therefore, assume that Job has sinned and is being punished. They encourage him to repent and assure him that God will make everything all right if he does. But in making that promise, they are using their "knowledge of God" to encourage Job to manipulate and even control God. Job rightly describes them as having "their god in their hand" (Job 12:6). Their god is little more than a genie who can give them what they want. This is their grave error. For them, "Who is God?" If we are using God to accomplish our own will, are we not making ourselves to be God?

Eventually God does come to Job—not with answers, but as someone to relate to. Job realizes that this is what he wanted, after all. Job moves through his suffering to know God better.

D. A. Carson well summarizes some of the key lessons of Job:

> The reason for suffering is not rooted in the past but in the future—it may not be punishment for past sins but is designed to develop our characters. . . . God is less interested in answering our questions than in other things: securing our allegiance, establishing our faith, nurturing a desire for holiness. An important part of spiritual maturity is bound up with this obvious truth. God tells us a great deal about himself; but the mysteries that remain are

74

not going to be answered at a merely theoretical and intellectual level. We may probe a little around the edges, using the minds God has given us to glimpse something of his glory. But ultimately the Christian will take refuge from questions about God not in proud, omniscient explanations but in adoring worship.[1]

Psalms

The book of Psalms also has much to teach us about dealing with the difficulties of life. Many Christians find comfort through individual psalms when their faith is challenged. How comforting it is to know that "the LORD is my shepherd . . ." (Ps. 23:1) and "God is our refuge and strength . . ." (Ps. 46:1). But we often fail to recognize that the entire book of Psalms was carefully edited to tell a simple story. Looking at the big picture, Psalms is divided into five books. Each of them ends with a doxology, a statement of praise to the Lord. The fifth book concludes with five psalms of praise (Psalms 146–150). The lesson of the Psalms is as profound as it is simple: even in light of the personal tragedies faced by the psalmists and the horrible losses that the Israelites endured, including the loss of their land and temple, they could still praise the Lord.

God's Character

To "rise above" our suffering, we must first understand God's character, and then why he permits us to suffer.

Strong and Loving. The Scriptures affirm that God is both strong and loving. So sang the psalmist:

> One thing God has spoken,
>   two things have I heard:
> that you, O God, are strong,
>   and that you, O LORD, are loving. . . . (Ps. 62:11–12, NIV)

When we are confronted with disease or death, when the doctor tells us that the biopsy showed cancer, our faith will be challenged. We may conclude that God was not strong enough to prevent a disease. Or we may choose to think that he did not love us enough to stop it. The psalmist affirms that God is both strong and loving. We must too. If we believe this, we will have to acknowledge that he had good reasons to allow the tragedy and we will trust him. In considering God's love we must understand that we are not to ground our understanding of God's love in how we perceive our present circumstances but in the cross of Jesus—in his suffering and death.

We may not always live to see how God is glorified through the suffering we endure. But ultimately, we believe he will be. What counts most is that no calamity can ever separate us from the love of God. Of this the apostle Paul boldly assures us: "that neither death nor life, nor angels nor rulers, nor things present nor things to come, nor powers, nor height nor depth, nor anything else in all creation, will be able to separate us from the love of God in Christ Jesus our Lord" (Rom. 8:38–39).

God may show his power and love for us by rescuing us from a tragedy. At other times he may choose to do so by giving us the grace to endure one.

The Scriptures make it clear that Satan is under our all-powerful God's sovereign control. Satan, the "prince of the power of the air" (Eph. 2:2), may bring evil our way, but he is not ultimately in control. He has been finally and totally defeated at the cross. Paul emphatically states: "And having disarmed the powers and authorities, [Christ] made a public spectacle of them, triumphing over them by the cross" (Col. 2:15, NIV). Though Satan is still active and can inflict great harm, his defeat has been secured. We are promised: "for he who is in you is greater than he who is in the world" (1 John 4:4).

All-knowing. Another attribute of God that we can count on when we are facing grave difficulties is that he is all-wise and all-knowing: Because God is omniscient, we can be confident that he knows exactly where we are in our character development and how to accomplish his purpose in us. In other words, we can be sure he knows what he is doing.

Also, because of his omniscience we can be confident he will never allow us to go through more than is necessary to accomplish his purpose in us. Paul wrote, "God is faithful, and he will not let you be tempted beyond your ability, but with the temptation he will also provide the way of escape, that you may be able to endure it" (1 Cor. 10:13).

Eternal. Scripture does not fully explain God's relationship to time. We do know that he does not move through time in the same way that we do. The psalmist wrote, "from everlasting to everlasting you are God" (Ps. 90:2). From time past to time future, God is in the present tense. Jesus himself made this clear when he said, "Truly, truly, I say to you, before Abraham was, I am" (John 8:58). The important lesson here is that while we are going through our lives, God can see the end result. Understanding God's eternal perspective allows us to share the unbeaten attitude of the apostle Paul, who wrote: "So we do not lose heart. Though our outer self is wasting away, our inner self is being renewed day by day. For this light momentary affliction is preparing for us an eternal weight of glory beyond all comparison, as we look not to the things that are seen but to the things that are unseen. For the things that are seen are transient, but the things that are unseen are eternal" (2 Cor. 4:16–18). Believers can go through trying circumstances by stepping back and looking at their difficulties from the perspective of our eternal God. That eternal perspective can be transforming.

Suffering. God has himself suffered in two ways. He has suffered as the man Jesus and he has suffered as a Father giving his Son to die. Because God has suffered, we can be confident that he knows what it is like to suffer; we can approach him as an understanding, loving Father as we pour out our hearts to him in our distress. We are appropriately distraught when we hear tragic stories of people dying young, but we must remember that Jesus not only suffered but also experienced an unnatural and, from a human point of view, untimely death.

Gracious. How grateful we must be that faith is a gift from God. He gives us saving faith: "For by grace you have been saved through faith. And this is not your own doing; it is the gift of God, not a result of works, so that no one may boast" (Eph. 2:8–9).

Similarly we cannot by ourselves generate a faith in God's grace that will bring us through the later challenges of our lives. Paul suffered some ailment that he referred to as his "thorn in the flesh." He summarized the lesson he learned from this experience by saying:

> But he said to me, "My grace is sufficient for you, for my power is made perfect in weakness." Therefore I will boast all the more gladly of my weaknesses, so that the power of Christ may rest upon me. For the sake of Christ, then, I am content with weaknesses, insults, hardships, persecutions, and calamities. For when I am weak, then I am strong. (2 Cor. 12:9–10)

It is by that daily provision of grace that God allows us to go through difficulties—for his glory.[2] We need to pray that he graciously allows us faith to endure. The more often we experience his grace the better prepared we will be to trust him for it in the future. In one sense death itself is our final opportunity to prove that God's grace is sufficient. The more we experience his grace in this life, the better prepared we will be to die.[3]

God's Purpose in Our Suffering
It Is God's Will That We Suffer
Our suffering does not take God by surprise. The apostle Peter clearly teaches that suffering is a part of God's will for us. He spoke of faithful Christians "who suffer according to God's will . . ." (1 Pet. 4:19). That does not mean we masochistically embrace suffering or even look forward to it. In the garden of Gethsemane, Jesus anticipated the suffering of the cross and prayed that it would not happen. Nevertheless, we are thankful that his desire to obey his Father was stronger than his aversion to suffering. He could pray: "Nevertheless, not my will, but yours, be done" (Luke 22:42). He knew that it was the Father's will for him to suffer, and he submitted.

Suffering was not a part of God's original good creation. It came as a result of the fall of the human race into sin. But as with other consequences of man's sin, God allows suffering and can accomplish his glory through it. Wherever we are in our lives, we can be confident that God has his purposes for us. The psalmist could say, "I cry out to God Most High, to God who fulfills his purpose for me" (Ps. 57:2). Quadriplegic Joni Eareckson Tada writes in *The God I Love*, "Sometimes God allows what he hates to accomplish what he loves."[4]

What are God's purposes in our suffering? We may not always know. We must simply choose to trust him. Whatever his immediate purpose is, we can be confident that his ultimate purpose is that he will be glorified. In that we can find great comfort. In the introduction I quoted Paul: "For from him and through him and to him are all things. To him be glory forever. Amen" (Rom. 11:36). We can take comfort that the "all things" in this passage include the very things that cause our suffering.

Scripture has much to say about the results that God can accomplish in our lives through suffering. Understanding the fruit that suffering can produce can help us endure.

Our Suffering Helps Others

God, in his sovereignty, can use the suffering of one person to teach others. We saw in the book of Job that God wanted to teach a lesson to Satan as well as to us. Peter taught that one Christian could be helped by knowing of the perseverance of another: "Resist him, firm in your faith, knowing that the same kinds of suffering are being experienced by your brotherhood throughout the world" (1 Pet. 5:9).

Scripture also makes it clear that our suffering may prepare us to give comfort to others. Paul recognized this purpose. God, he wrote, "comforts us in all our affliction, so that we may be able to comfort those who are in any affliction, with the comfort with which we ourselves are comforted by God" (2 Cor. 1:4).

Suffering Can Demonstrate God's Work

God might use our suffering to demonstrate his healing power to accomplish his glory. This truth is embodied in the case of the blind man in John's gospel: "And his disciples asked, 'Rabbi, who sinned, this man or his parents, that he was born blind?' Jesus answered, 'It was not that this man sinned, or his parents, but that the works of God might be displayed in him'" (John 9:2–3). We see the same evidenced in the case of Lazarus (see John 11). Jesus knew that Lazarus was dying and that he could have gotten there before Lazarus died, in time to heal him. Jesus chose instead to arrive on the fourth day after Lazarus died. It appears that Jesus' purpose was to allow Lazarus to die with all of the grief and sadness that death brings so that God would be glorified by Lazarus being raised from the dead.

Experiencing God's deliverance from suffering will confirm that God is at work in us. He knows we may need this kind of deliverance to be an anchor for our faith. Note how Peter affirms this:

> In this you rejoice, though now for a little while, if necessary, you have been grieved by various trials, so that the tested genuineness of your faith—more precious than gold that perishes though it is tested by fire—may be found to result in praise and glory and honor at the revelation of Jesus Christ. (1 Pet. 1:6–7)

Through suffering we may learn more of God's love and faithfulness. Think back for a moment to Job. I suspect that before Satan's onslaught, Job would honestly have said that he believed "God was good." That statement would have been honest yet untested. However, if Job said the very same thing in chapter 42, after persevering through the awful things he had endured, it would be much more profound and meaningful. Job's experience of God's grace gave him a clearer view of God.

God May Use Suffering to Transform Our Character
God has an agenda for us. His goal is to work in us to make us into the people he wants us to be. The author of the book of Hebrews explains how God, as a loving Father, disciplines us: "It is for discipline that you have to endure. God is treating you as sons. For what son is there whom his father does not discipline? If you are left without discipline, in which all have participated, then you are illegitimate children and not sons" (Heb. 12:7–8).

Even when discipline is not involved, God can work through the difficulties of our lives to transform us:

> More than that, we rejoice in our sufferings, knowing that suffering produces endurance, and endurance produces character, and character produces hope, and hope does not put us to shame, because God's love has been poured into our hearts through the Holy Spirit who has been given to us. (Rom. 5:3–5)

His methods are the best for us, but they are not always easy. I find that many believers love the image of God as the potter and us as clay:

> But now, O LORD, you are our Father;
>> we are the clay, and you are our potter;
>> we are all the work of your hand. (Isa. 64:8)

I wonder how many of us would volunteer to be plopped down on a wheel and spun around at 250 rpm while our rough edges are knocked off. On the other hand who would we trust more to do it than our loving heavenly Father?

Part of our character formation is helping us to develop a greater aversion to sin in our lives. To use the old phrase, suffering may *mortify the flesh*: "Since therefore Christ suffered in the flesh, arm yourselves with the same way of thinking, for whoever has suffered in the flesh has ceased from sin, so as to live for the rest of the time in the flesh no longer for human passions but for the will of God" (1 Pet. 4:1–2).

Indeed, one of the sins that we must commonly confront is pride. Paul described his experience this way: "So to keep me from becoming conceited because of the surpassing greatness of the revelations, a thorn was given me in the flesh, a messenger of Satan to harass me, to keep me from becoming conceited" (2 Cor. 12:7).

As we become less prideful, we may depend more on God. One striking example comes out of the atrocities of the Nazi regime:

Bless my enemies, O Lord. Even I bless them and do not curse them. Enemies have driven me into your embrace more than friends have. Friends have bound me to earth, enemies have loosed me from earth and have demolished all my aspirations in the world. Enemies have made me a stranger in worldly realms and an extraneous inhabitant of the world. Just as a hunted animal finds safer shelter than an unhunted animal does, so have I, persecuted by enemies, found the safest sanctuary, having ensconced myself beneath your tabernacle, where neither friends nor enemies can slay my soul. Bless my enemies, O Lord. Even I bless and do not curse them.[5]

In the book *Holy Living and Dying*, Jeremy Taylor, a nineteenth-century pastor, wrote of some of the results of sickness: "It takes off the fancies of vanity, it attempers the spirit, it cures hypocrisy, it tames the fumes of pride, it is the school of patience, and by taking us from off the brisker relishes of the world, it makes us with more gust to taste the things of the Spirit."[6] He may not use the same words we would, but he expresses a profound truth.

God may use suffering toward the end of life to wean us from our love of this world. We may have taken great pride in our physical strength and appearance, but as we age and experience more pain and suffering, our bodies become more like prisons. We may long to be free, and a glorified body in heaven looks very attractive.

Paul and Peter say similar things about the relationship between suffering and future glory:

And if children, then heirs—heirs of God and fellow heirs with Christ, provided we suffer with him in order that we may also be glorified with him.

For I consider that the sufferings of this present time are not worth comparing with the glory that is to be revealed to us. (Rom. 8:17–18)

But rejoice insofar as you share Christ's sufferings, that you may also rejoice and be glad when his glory is revealed. (1 Pet. 4:13)

Suffering may allow us to experience God's glory in deeper and richer ways, which is why Paul says that present suffering is not worth comparing to future glory.

Suffering May Be a Punishment for Sin

There are times when God allows suffering not just to transform our characters but also to be a direct punishment for wrongs in our lives. An example of this is in 1 Corinthians 11:29–30, where an abuse of the Lord's Supper caused some to become weak and ill, and even to die.

Suffering Provides Deeper Fellowship with Jesus

I've had many opportunities to see the benefit of having others share in a person's suffering. One of the most difficult tasks of being a doctor is giving a patient bad news. It's been my practice to ask the patient's loved ones to be with me when I have to do so. At such times, the presence of others makes bad news easier to accept. The daughter may begin to cry; the son may say, "Mom it will be okay"; or the husband might simply squeeze his wife's hand. One way or another, Mom knows that the people she loves are with her and that as they feel her pain, she feels it less. Suffering is something we can share.

In a far greater way we can share our suffering with Jesus and with the Holy Spirit. In Philippians 3:10 Paul refers to our sharing in the sufferings of Jesus. The word for share is *koinonia*, which is most commonly translated "fellowship." It is good for us to appreciate more fully what Jesus endured on the cross for us. But fellowship is a two-way street; he has suffered for us, and we will likely be called upon to suffer for him. As we share in his sufferings, he will be there to share in ours. Hebrews says: "For we do not have a high priest who is unable to sympathize with our weaknesses, but one who in every respect has been tempted as we are, yet without sin. Let us then with confidence draw near to the throne of grace, that we may receive mercy and find grace to help in time of need" (Heb. 4:15–16). Jesus knows what it is like to suffer physically and emotionally. As a result he will be sympathetic to us when we come to him to request his help to get through. Not only that, there are two additional astounding truths. First, even before we come to him he is already interceding with the Father for us (Rom. 8:34; Heb. 7:25). Second, he has sent the Holy Spirit to be with us. In the Greek New Testament he is referred to as our *paraklete* (John 14:26; 15:26; 16:7). That is a word that could be translated helper, counselor, comforter, or intercessor. When we suffer, Jesus and the Holy Spirit will be with us to help. I have learned that some of the people I am closest to in this life are those I have gone through times of difficulty with. When we experience the presence of God in our suffering, we will be drawn closer to him.

Suffering May Be God's Way to Take Us to Heaven

Sometimes God chooses to bring his children home through suffering. When I told my friend Edie that she had terminal cancer, she responded rather incredulously, "Well you don't get to heaven by being healthy, do you?" Suffering may be our last experience of this sin-cursed world as God takes us to be with himself. Once we are in God's presence, we may be able to look back and marvel at the way God delivered us from our suffering, but I do not believe we will spend much time thinking about the anguish of this life. I cannot imagine this conversation in heaven: "I got here by pancreatic cancer." "Is that so? I came through a plane crash." No, the means God uses to take us home will be totally irrelevant. What will consume our thinking is that we are in heaven by God's grace because Jesus paid the penalty of our sins.

We Can Help Others Find God's Purpose in Their Suffering

That God has purposes for our suffering is a consoling truth to keep in mind when we try to reach out to those who are suffering. However, these may not be "teachable moments." Recall the book of Job. When Job's three friends came to console him, they sat in silence for seven days before they said anything. Their presence was most comforting. But then when they started to talk and explain their theological understanding of Job's suffering, they did nothing but cause Job more distress. I am fully aware that when my patients call me to relieve their pain, they do not want a theological explanation for their suffering; they want something to stop the pain and they want it now. Sometimes, however, in addition to relieving pain, it may be appropriate to remind them of God's purposes. I might read the above Scriptures with them, and we might talk together about the way God is using their present difficulties to accomplish his purposes to prepare them for the glories of heaven. At times I can ask my patients what the Lord is doing in their inner spirit and how they are responding to him. I must be careful not do to this with glib platitudes but to always be sensitive to the emotional context.

Our Response to Pain and Suffering

Being a Christian offers a valuable asset during times of duress: hope. Clinging to this asset enabled Paul to face successfully all sorts of difficulties:

> For I consider that the sufferings of this present time are not worth comparing with the glory that is to be revealed to us. . . . For in this hope we were saved. Now hope that is seen is not hope. For who hopes for what he sees? But if we hope for what we do not see, we wait for it with patience. (Rom. 8:18, 24–25)

No matter what their current situation, Christians can anticipate a better day. Though it may not occur in this life, it will eventually. We anticipate a future that will be far greater than anything we have ever known on earth—a future that will make the difficulties of this life seem like mere trifles.

We take as our model in this the Lord Jesus himself, of whom it was said: "who for the joy that was set before him endured the cross, despising the shame, and is seated at the right hand of the throne of God" (Heb. 12:2). That hope of a better future frequently enables us to keep going when we might otherwise despair.

Christians Can Mingle Suffering with Joy

While we as believers may have some insight into God's purposes in our suffering and find great consolation in those purposes, the hope we have does not erase the deep agony we sometimes feel. Recall how Job tore his robe and shaved his head upon hearing of all of his losses before he fell on the ground and worshiped. Believing in a sovereign God does not diminish the weight of the grief we feel. Yet, by faith we can mingle our suffering with joy as we rest unquestionably in God's promises and his justness. Isn't this what it means to "rejoice in the Lord always . . ." (Phil. 4:4)? We need not be in denial. We can accept our suffering, for we have a deep reason for hope. Horatio Spafford captured it so well in his hymn:

> When peace, like a river, attendeth my way,
> When sorrows like sea billows roll;
> Whatever my lot, thou has taught me to say,
> "It is well, it is well, with my soul."[7]

What If We Feel God Is Unfair?

I have presented an idealistic response to pain and suffering. The only problem is that we do not always respond to our trials with great faith or joy. Sometimes we feel the agony but we do not respond with joy; sometimes we cannot say "it is well" with our souls. The pain hurts badly, and the suffering gets to us. Our sense of fairness and rightness have been offended. We begin to feel that God is not absolutely in control, or if he is, he is not as loving and kind as we had believed. These are very real emotions and should not be denied. When we feel this way, we have every right to cry out to God and to plead with him to respond. We see this repeatedly in the Psalms. I love when the psalmist cries out, "Awake! Why are you sleeping, O Lord? Rouse yourself! Do not reject us forever!" (Ps. 44:23). This was not blasphemy but an honest plea to God. Many psalms are laments decrying the horrible situation that befell the writer.

When we are in such distress, we can cry out to God in two ways. One is to be like the little boy who stomps his foot and shouts at his mother, "But that's not fair!" He is looking only from his perspective, and putting his own sense of fairness above that of the mom. When we respond that way to God, are we not saying that we know more than God and trying to be God ourselves? Does that not bring us right back to the sin of Adam in the garden? The other response is in all humility to cry out to God for relief, asking him to give us some glimpse into his purpose in our suffering, pleading with him to give us the faith to persevere, and continuing to cling to him with all of the faith he allows us. When we respond in that way, we give him his rightful place and allow God to be God.

Conclusion

While pain and suffering are the result of Adam's fall into sin, they were not part of God's original good creation. Still, God allows us to suffer and will accomplish good results through our suffering. We can go through times of suffering confident that God will accomplish his purposes, and we can anticipate better things to come. In this way we can allow adversity to draw us closer to God, and we can grow through it.

Prayer

Dear Father, the thought of suffering scares me. I cannot say that I look forward to it. Yet, Father, I trust you. If my future includes suffering, I know that you will either bring me through it or give me the grace to endure to the end. My highest priority is not my comfort but my faithfulness and obedience to you. I pray this for the glory of your name. Amen.

=== MEDITATION ===

My life is but a weaving
Between the Lord and me;

I may not choose the colors—
He knows what they should be.

For he can view the pattern
Upon the upper side
While I can see it only
On this, the underside.

Sometimes he weaves in sorrow,
Which seems so strange to me;
But I will trust his judgment
And work on faithfully.

'Tis he who fills the shuttle,
And he knows what is best;
So I shall weave in earnest,
And leave to him the rest.

Not 'til the loom is silent
And the shuttles cease to fly
Shall God unroll the canvas
And explain the reason why.

The dark threads are as needed
In the Weaver's skillful hand
As the threads of gold and silver
In the pattern he has planned.

*THE PLAN OF THE
MASTER WEAVER,*
AUTHOR UNKNOWN

Embrace a Biblical View of Life and Death

What does the Bible teach about life and death?

What does death lead to?

How do we balance the truth that death is an enemy, but it is a defeated enemy?

Does God determine the time of our death?

The terms *death* and *dying* arouse many different emotions. Many people recoil when they hear them and want to change the subject. I saw this when I gave a series of lectures that my church sponsored. We announced four sessions on the issues of aging on four Sunday afternoons. I was thrilled when about 250 people came to three of the talks, but disappointed and surprised when only about 60 attended the talk about dying. Several of my friends told me they chose not to attend that one simply because they found it uncomfortable to think about dying. I also saw this negative response to thinking about death in Susie, a woman who had over and over come to death's door, but each time had survived against the odds. I saw her when she was struggling in the intensive care unit and did not appear to be far from death. I felt it was appropriate for her to agree to a "do not resuscitate" order, since I knew that soon she would suffer a cardiac arrest. An attempted resuscitation would not likely succeed and it could give her a difficult end. I felt Susie understood what I was advising her, but after I finished, she gave me a broad smile and said, "I really like your tie!" Talk about denial. In one sense I understand; we want to ignore death and deny it will come. But in another sense, it was tragic. If we do not understand death in biblical terms, it is impossible to make wise, God-honoring decisions as the end of life approaches. Therefore I want to talk to you about strategy 5: Embrace a Biblical View of Life and Death.

Theology of Life
To comprehend the meaning of death, we must first understand life. You will recall the circle of God's holiness that I presented earlier. Life belongs in that circle. It was part of the original creation that God called "good." The apostle John gives us a further understanding of life when in the prologue to his Gospel he speaks of Jesus as the Creator and then affirms, "In him was life . . ." (John 1:4). However we understand life, we must take into account that the Scriptures teach that life is intrinsic to Jesus. The apostle Paul put it this way: "In him we live and move and have our being" (Acts 17:28). Quite simply, there is no life apart from Jesus.

Life can be understood on a variety of different levels. First there is the simple life of a cell; then there are the more complex organisms of plants and then animals. The highest order of physical life has been allotted to humans. Our lives are distinct from all other life in that we are made in the image of God: "So God created man in his own image, in the image of God he created him; male and female he created them" (Gen. 1:27). Being made in the image of God is a profound concept, the full force of which we will not try to develop here. Suffice it to say, being God's image-bearers sets all of humanity apart from other life forms. The terminally ill, those whose bodies are wracked with horrible diseases, and yes, even those whose minds are severely demented are all made in the image of God. Further, human life comes directly from God: "Then the LORD God formed the man of dust from the ground and breathed into his nostrils the breath of life, and the man became a living creature" (Gen. 2:7), "since he himself gives to all mankind life and breath and everything" (Acts 17:25). Our physical life is a precious gift that God has given to us. But everything that he gives, he holds us accountable for. The book of Genesis makes that clear: "And for your lifeblood I will require a reckoning: from every beast I will require it and from man. From his fellow man I will require a reckoning for the life of man. 'Whoever sheds the blood of man, by man shall his blood be shed, for God made man in his own image'" (Gen. 9:5–6). Truly there is sanctity to life.

These theological truths emphasize the value of our physical lives, but a fuller understanding of what the Bible says about life makes our appreciation of it even richer. Later in his Gospel John writes: "And this is eternal life, that they know you the only true God, and Jesus Christ whom you have sent" (John 17:3). Now John is talking about life on the highest possible plane. This is life in relationship with a personal, loving God. We were made to find our fulfillment in nothing less than the infinite resources of God himself. We refer to this as spiritual life, or life in fellowship with God. Jesus said, "I came that they may have life and have it abundantly" (John 10:10). Spiritual life begins while we are living on this earth, but we will not experience its fullness till we are free from sin in the presence of God; then we will enjoy it through all eternity. We err when we overemphasize the value of physical life at the expense of our life with God.

Theology of Death
Once we understand life in biblical terms, we are ready to see what Scripture has to say about death. Just as life is both phys-

ical and spiritual, so is death. There is physical death that leads to a separation from this world, and there is spiritual death that involves separation from God. When we are born physically, we are spiritually dead. If, in this life, we believe in and trust our eternal well-being to Jesus, God by his Spirit enters into us and we become spiritually alive. Then when we die physically, we remain spiritually alive forever and ever. If we do not come to trust Jesus while we are alive on earth, we will remain separated from God.

Death Is an Enemy

While life is a part of God's original creation, within the circle of his holiness, death is outside the circle and results from sin. Death can be ugly and nasty. Indeed, in 1 Corinthians 15:26 Paul says death is an enemy.

Jan's father was eighty-three. He was becoming more demented and would soon be unable to live at home. One day he was hospitalized for chest pain, though he did not want aggressive care. The first night he was in the hospital, he apparently got up on his own, collapsed, and died. Jan came to my office to tell me about it. She wanted to tell me how grateful she was for his life, that he died quickly without suffering, and, in her words, how "beautiful" it all was. Yet she was in tears. She had lost her dad. I agreed from a narrow perspective that one could see his death as being more "beautiful" than the deaths of those who die in their prime or of lingering, painful diseases. But still Jan cried. Why? Because she, too, was keenly aware that death is an enemy. It does not belong to God's holiness, and it separated a father from his loving daughter. Even a "beautiful death" has its tragic elements. Some deaths have very little that is beautiful. I think of the pastor who died leaving a pregnant wife. Not only did a church lose their shepherd but a son was raised never knowing his father's love. I remember Patsy, who, having been part of a story-book romance, died a week before she was to be married. One would be in stark denial to say that those deaths were beautiful.

Because of all the troublesome things that accompany death, people often fear it. That is why Jesus came to "deliver all those who through fear of death were subject to lifelong slavery" (Heb. 2:15). I have often seen people express fear of dying. Alice, for instance, suffered from kidney failure near the end of her life, and she was mildly confused. Lying in her nursing home bed she cried out over and over again: "I'm afraid to die! Don't let me die!" It was unsettling for those of us caring for her to hear this agonizing cry hour after hour. She had been told the good news of Jesus; whether she had accepted it or not only God knows. Still she had this terrible fear of death that ravished her right up till the end.

It is appropriate for believers to react strongly to death; we have no reason to love it or speak kindly of it. The diseases and losses that lead up to death are horrible. "I hate death" is an appropriate thing to say—even for Christians. Recall Jesus weeping at the tomb of Lazarus even though he knew that he would raise him from the dead (John 11:35). Jesus did not weep because Lazarus was dead; he cried because of what death had done to his good creation.[1]

We should be inspired by Paul's testimony that he looked forward to dying and being with Christ. He could say "to die is gain" (Phil. 1:21). On the other hand it is intriguing that in the very next chapter he speaks of Epaphroditis's being sick and close to death. Paul considered it a mercy from God that Epaphroditis had not died, for that would have caused Paul "sorrow upon sorrow." Certainly Paul considered death an enemy.

Since death is an enemy, we must never consider it a friend. Life is a precious gift from God, and we must be good stewards of it. But thank God for the fact that death is an enemy is balanced by the truth that it is a defeated enemy.

Death Is a Defeated Enemy
We will be eternally grateful that God did not allow our enemy, death, to be the ultimate victor. Rather, God promises that in the end, life will win.

When the perishable puts on the imperishable, and the mortal puts on immortality, then shall come to pass the saying that is written:

"Death is swallowed up in victory."
"O death, where is your victory?
 O death, where is your sting?"

The sting of death is sin, and the power of sin is the law. But thanks be to God, who gives us the victory through our Lord Jesus Christ. (1 Cor. 15:54–57)

These astounding words describe the difference between eternal separation from God and eternal joy in his presence. Through the death and resurrection of Jesus, death, which was outside the circle of God's holiness and had been the reigning principle over life, has been destroyed, allowing "those who receive the abundance of grace and the free gift of righteousness [to] reign in life . . ." (Rom. 5:17). We are back in the circle of God's holiness. Death is no longer simply an enemy, but is now a defeated enemy. Defeated enemies are not necessarily friends, but they do not hold ultimate power; they need not be feared. As a result of Christ's death, "There is therefore now no condemnation for those who are in Christ Jesus" (Rom. 8:1); a believer's physical death no longer leads to punishment.

Because the significance of dying is different for Christians, the Bible avoids using the term "death" to refer to death of believers. It uses metaphors such as sleeping, changing our clothes, or moving from a tent into a permanent house.[2]

Death Leads to Receiving Our Reward
Thanks to Christ's redeeming work, death, our defeated enemy, is now used by God to accomplish his loving purpose toward us. Unless the second coming of Christ intervenes, the only way to our eternal future with God is through death. In spite of all of the nastiness, ugliness, separations, and sadness associated with death, it can still lead to rejoicing for the Christian. God uses

death to call us into his presence. "Yes, we are of good courage, and we would rather be away from the body and at home with the Lord" (2 Cor. 5:8). Murray Harris emphasizes that this is not simply a statement about geography—physically we will be in God's presence—but it is also a statement about relationship. We will experience a higher degree of fellowship with the Lord in heaven than we have ever been able to have on earth.[3]

We will enjoy not only God's presence, but all of his other blessings as well. I once heard Charles Swindoll say on the radio that when a godly person dies, nothing that is truly of God ever perishes. For example, we can confidently anticipate the day when we will be reunited with our believing loved ones, both those who have already died and those who will come after us. God is the author of all of the beauty that we enjoy on this earth, and we can be confident that he will continue to share with us the results of his creative genius.

We will also have peace. When dying transports us into God's presence, we will enter our eternal rest: "'Blessed are the dead who die in the Lord from now on.' 'Blessed indeed,' says the Spirit, 'that they may rest from their labors . . .'" (Rev. 14:13). When we enter the presence of the Lord, we will finally have what we had hoped for—and even more.

C. S. Lewis has captured this spirit so well at the conclusion of the Narnia tales:

> "There was a real railway accident," said Aslan softly. "Your father and mother and all of you are—as you used to call it in the Shadow-Lands—dead. The term is over: the holidays have begun. The dream is ended: this is the morning." And as He spoke He no longer looked to them like a lion, but the things that began to happen after that were so great and beautiful that I cannot write them. And for us this is the end of all the stories, and we can most truly say that they all lived happily ever after. But for them it was only the beginning of the real story. All their life in this world and all their adventures in Narnia had only been the cover and the title page: now at last they were beginning Chapter One of the Great

Story, which no one on earth has read: which goes on for ever: in which every chapter is better than the one before."[4]

Death Leads to a Resurrection Body

While we live on earth, it is not uncommon that the limitations of our physical bodies interfere with our being able to experience God's love to the fullest. We long for glorified bodies that will far exceed our present bodies in their ability to enjoy God. An unavoidable lesson of aging is that our bodies are wearing out. My good friend, New Testament scholar Grant Osborne, commented, "The older I get the more I know my body hates me." As age and disease take their toll, we may begin to groan, and then it is only natural for us to long for something better. Paul wrote, "And not only the creation, but we ourselves, who have the firstfruits of the Spirit, groan inwardly as we wait eagerly for adoption as sons, the redemption of our bodies" (Rom. 8:23). It is the redemption of the body that we must wait for with patience.

I doubt that many truly understand the consequences of the fall on our physical bodies. We also have little inkling of what the promised eternal resurrected body will be like; yet Scripture says a fair amount about it. Paul wrote: "Just as we have borne the image of the man of dust, we shall also bear the image of the man of heaven" (1 Cor. 15:49). We presently live in a physical body that is similar to that of our first father, Adam, after the devastation caused by sin. We can look forward to a new body, which is in the image of the Lord Jesus himself. Our resurrected bodies will have some of the characteristics of our earthly bodies, but in other ways our bodies will be more like that of the resurrected Christ. After his resurrection, Christ had recognizable physical characteristics: he could be touched, eat food, and walk from place to place. In other ways he was wholly different from before. He appeared in a room whose doors were shut and secured. In some unknown way he was transported from Jerusalem to Galilee. From these biblical accounts we can conclude that once we are resurrected, as Christ was, there will be some continuity between our present bodies and our resurrected bodies, but there will be differences as well.

Paul uses an analogy to explain how magnificent the body God has in store for us will be: "And what you sow is not the body that is to be, but a bare kernel, perhaps of wheat or of some other grain" (1 Cor. 15:37). Suppose the kernel is corn. What a vast difference there is between it and the full stalk that will eventually grow from it. While it is true that the kernel contains all of the potential to become a tree, all comparisons stop there. The one is puny and insignificant; it is buried in the ground, and then grows to its full potential. So will be the difference between our present physical bodies and the resurrected body we will receive.

Resurrection will restore to us what it means to be truly human and equip us for God's glorious presence. It will allow our bodies to return to the circle of God's holiness. All of the physical devastations caused by the fall into sin will be removed. In these new bodies we will never again experience disease or sorrow—and most importantly, there will be no more death: "He will wipe away every tear from their eyes, and death shall be no more, neither shall there be mourning nor crying nor pain anymore, for the former things have passed away" (Rev. 21:4). This prospect should electrify us.

Death Leads to Judgment

Alas, not only does reward follow dying, but judgment does as well: "And just as it is appointed for man to die once, and after that comes judgment" (Heb. 9:27). The Bible teaches that there will be two types of judgment. The purpose of the first is to determine who will go to heaven and who will go to hell. This is a reality we would all prefer not to think about, but the Bible makes it very clear:

> When the Son of Man comes in his glory, and all the angels with him, then he will sit on his glorious throne. Before him will be gathered all the nations, and he will separate people one from another as a shepherd separates the sheep from the goats. And he will place the sheep on his right, but the goats on the left.

Then the King will say to those on his right, "Come, you who are blessed by my Father, inherit the kingdom prepared for you from the foundation of the world. . . . Then he will say to those on his left, 'Depart from me, you cursed, into the eternal fire prepared for the devil and his angels'" (Matt. 25:31–34, 41).

Yes, a day of judgment is coming. God's verdict on some will be condemnation to eternal suffering and banishment from his presence. Having chosen to live their lives without God, they will be granted their desire. But at that same judgment some will be welcomed into God's kingdom—a privilege they did not earn. Though some are condemned to hell because of their evil deeds, it is not because of good works that others are destined to eternal life. To be with God forever requires being wholly sinless, which none of us is: "for all have sinned and fall short of the glory of God" (Rom. 3:23). No amount of good works can counterbalance our condition of being sinful. Sin condemns us to a death that is an eternal separation from God: "For the wages of sin is death, but the free gift of God is eternal life in Christ Jesus our Lord" (Rom. 6:23). What spares us from this death is what Jesus provides for those who trust in him. Having lived a sinless life, he did not need to die for his own sin but died to satisfy God's judgment against the sins of the whole world: "For our sake he made him to be sin who knew no sin, so that in him we might become the righteousness of God" (2 Cor. 5:21).

God will not accept Christ's payment for our sins unless we are willing to do so ourselves. We must humbly acknowledge that we are sinners, repent of our sin, confess that we do not deserve what he has done for us and that we cannot earn it, but then believe that Jesus's death has paid for our sins and ask God's forgiveness. God then accepts Christ's death as payment for our sins and welcomes us into his presence. It is his grace, not our goodness, that makes this possible.

There is another day of judgment coming as well. This will be for those who have believed in Christ and will be in heaven. Here, too, Jesus will be the judge. There will be no threat of eternal punishment; the focus will be on reward, not punishment:

> Now if anyone builds on the foundation with gold, silver, precious stones, wood, hay, straw—each one's work will become manifest, for the Day will disclose it, because it will be revealed by fire, and the fire will test what sort of work each one has done. If the work that anyone has built on the foundation survives, he will receive a reward. If anyone's work is burned up, he will suffer loss, though he himself will be saved, but only as through fire. (1 Cor. 3:12–15)

All of our works basically fall into three categories: sinful deeds, good deeds, and neutral deeds. When Christians stand before God as their judge, no record of their sins will be there because Christ paid for them by his death; they will be erased. However, many of the frivolous things we have done will be recalled and declared to have no lasting value. They will be treated as wood, hay, and straw and consumed by fire. They, too, will be gone. What will be left are the deeds that we have done for God, through the power of the Holy Spirit. They are likened to gold, silver, and precious stones, and they will last for all eternity. It is in view of this judgment that the Scriptures repeatedly exhort us to good works.

God Controls Death

That death is outside of the circle of God's holiness does not mean that he does not sovereignly control it. He knows the length of our lives from before we are born. He knows how, where, and when we will die. David could say:

> Your eyes saw my unformed substance;
> in your book were written, every one of them,
>   the days that were formed for me,
>   when as yet there were none of them. (Ps. 139:16)

Job echoes a similar thought:

> Since his days are determined,

and the number of his months is with you,
and you have appointed his limits that he cannot pass.
   (Job 14:5)

Patients often ask how long they have to live. I am fully aware of the studies that demonstrate how poorly doctors do at making such predictions. One of my frequent responses is simply, "I don't know. But I do know that there is a book up in heaven with your name in it and a date beside it." We can live peacefully knowing that truth.

In a very real sense death is not fundamentally caused by illness or the cessation of a physical process. Death is ultimately determined by God. When filling out death certificates, I am often tempted to simply write on the first line where one indicates the cause of death: "God called his child home." I haven't been brave enough to do it (and I don't think the health department would accept it), but it is the truth, isn't it?

We might believe that death is in God's control and he uses it to accomplish his purposes, but it is possible to use this truth insensitively. The death of a child, a newlywed, or a young parent is tragic, no matter how much we believe in God's sovereignty. These events should lead to deep grief. Job gives us an appropriate model. Though his initial response to the losses he endured, including the loss of his ten children, was very pious, he proceeded to wrestle for months with his feelings. Finally, after all of his soul-searching and time in God's presence, he was able to conclude: "I know that you can do all things, and that no purpose of yours can be thwarted" (Job 42:2). Job was able to acknowledge the sovereignty of God over his suffering. It is fairly easy to speak about the death of someone who led a full life as "God taking him home." We must be honest though and admit that it is much more difficult to respond to a death that we view as being premature (such as that of a teenager). When I encounter these situations, I pray that eventually the survivors will be able to recognize the good and loving hand of God in a profound way. It may take years to do so.

An obvious question raised by our belief that God is sovereign over death is: "Why should we fight against death if God is in control?" My best answer is that even while we accept God's sovereignty over our life and death, we still must make the wisest choices possible. We want to be so in tune with God that his sovereignty works through our choices. All human life is precious, and we must handle it with utmost respect. I, as a physician, want to do everything that is reasonable to uphold life until it is clear that God has decreed it to be over. Yet, even while I am pro-life, I must not be anti-death. The Bible teaches two potentially conflicting truths that we must hold in balance. One is that human life is sacred and we want to preserve it; death is an enemy. The other is that we will not experience the fullness of spiritual life until we are with the Lord in heaven; death is a defeated enemy. The challenge is knowing when to use aggressive medical care to preserve physical life, and when to accept that God is calling us home (and therefore to accept that we ought to prepare to peacefully enter his presence). That is the tension we struggle with and on which much of the rest of this book focuses.

Conclusion

Perhaps there is no better summary of a biblical view on death and aging than what the apostle Paul wrote to the Corinthians:

> For we know that if the tent that is our earthly home is destroyed, we have a building from God, a house not made with hands, eternal in the heavens. For in this tent we groan, longing to put on our heavenly dwelling, if indeed by putting it on we may not be found naked. For while we are still in this tent, we groan, being burdened—not that we would be unclothed, but that we would be further clothed, so that what is mortal may be swallowed up by life. He who has prepared us for this very thing is God, who has given us the Spirit as a guarantee.
>
> So we are always of good courage. We know that while we are at home in the body we are away from the Lord, for we walk by faith, not by sight. Yes, we are of good courage, and we would

rather be away from the body and at home with the Lord. So whether we are at home or away, we make it our aim to please him. For we must all appear before the judgment seat of Christ, so that each one may receive what is due for what he has done in the body, whether good or evil. (2 Cor. 5:1–10)

How crucial it is to have a clear theological understanding of both life and death. Physical life is of great value, but of still greater value is our eternal life with God in heaven.

Prayer
Sovereign Lord, I bless you for the life that you have given me. I am grateful that true life does not end at death. If that were the case, I would be sorely disappointed. You have provided for eternal life, and I long for that. I know that short of the return of the Lord Jesus, you will someday lead me to yourself through death. I do not look forward to my physical death, but I want to trust you. Give me the faith to trust you more. This I pray, for the sake of your great glory. Amen.

═══════════ MEDITATION ═══════════

Abide with me; fast falls the eventide;
The darkness deepens; Lord with me abide.
When other helpers fail and comforts flee,
Help of the helpless, O abide with me.

Swift to its close ebbs out life's little day;
Earth's joys grow dim; its glories pass away;
Change and decay in all around I see;
O thou who changest not, abide with me.

I need thy presence every passing hour.
What but thy grace can foil the tempter's power?

Who, like thyself, my guide and stay can be?
Through cloud and sunshine, Lord, abide with me.

I fear no foe, with thee at hand to bless;
Ills have no weight, and tears no bitterness.
Where is death's sting? Where, grave, thy victory?
I triumph still, if thou abide with me.

Hold thou thy cross before my closing eyes;
Shine through the gloom and point me to the skies.
Heaven's morning breaks, and earth's vain shadows flee;
In life, in death, O Lord, abide with me.

"Abide with Me," Henry Lyte (1847)

Complete Your Agenda

Can I have peace with myself when I die?

How do I relate to God in my final days on earth?

What needs to be done to bring closure with loved ones?

How do I leave a spiritual legacy?

How can my family be stronger when I am gone?

W hen I started medical school in the late sixties, sudden death was the rule of the day. Chicago would have a heavy snowstorm. The stalwart would go out to shovel snow and keel over, the heart unable to handle the strain. If people were nearby, they would run to the nearest phone and call the fire department. Firefighters would arrive to take the sufferer to the hospital, performing mouth-to-mouth resuscitation on the way. But little could actually be done to preserve the person's life until he or she was inside the emergency room. Most commonly, the victim was DOA (dead on arrival), sudden death having claimed yet another victim.

Thankfully, this course of events doesn't occur as often today because of a well-known telephone number: 911.

Upon seeing someone in a life-threatening situation, an alert person quickly pushes three keys on a handy cell phone, setting in motion a set of amazing life-saving procedures. Paramedics follow electronic instructions to get them to the side of the ailing person by the quickest route possible. These trained professionals arrive at the scene in a well-equipped mobile intensive care unit, essentially bringing the emergency room to the patient. Within moments of their arrival, using a portable defibrillator, they shock the dying person's heart, starting the blood to circulate before permanent damage is done to the heart or brain. Once at the hospital, the patient is transported to a waiting heart catheterization lab where the blocked artery is identified and a wire is passed through the offending clot. Soon a balloon is inserted over the wire and inflated to restore circulation. Finally, a small stent is often inserted to help ensure the artery will not close again. That same patient who would have been dead on arrival in 1970 is back at work in a week. Then twenty years later he becomes a victim of lung cancer because he did not stop smoking. He dies a slow death.[1]

Whether you look at the statistics for heart attacks, strokes, gunshot wounds, or car accidents, sudden death has become less common. More and more of us will need to adjust to our deaths coming slowly and gradually. This will not be easy, since modern people prefer their lives to end quickly; we tend to fear the process of dying more than we do death. Woody Allen quipped: "I don't mind dying, I just don't want to be around when it happens." Strangely, this modern preference wasn't always true for people. A century and a half ago, people feared the opposite, preferring a slow rather than quick death. The Anglican Book of Common Prayer includes the line, "Lord prevent us from sudden death." Apparently, people of the past believed that dying slowly had rewards that a sudden death did not, advantages that those of us today would do well to reclaim. Having some time between when we recognize we will soon die and when it actually happens can provide opportunities to bring closure to this life, making our death easier for our loved ones and giving us time to prepare for the next life.

If we are to have a good death, we must have a clear understanding of the things that need to be done before we die. To make this point when I am speaking to groups about aging and dying, I often ask them to list four of the most important events that have occurred between the time they were born and the present. Most can do that rather easily. Then I ask them to list four of the most important things that must take place between the present and when they will die. That is more challenging. Certainly it can be tragic to receive a terminal diagnosis and know you are near life's end. But despite the dreadfulness, this time can be quite meaningful if you know what you need to accomplish during it. This leads us to our next strategy to finish life well: strategy 6: Complete Your Agenda. I would like to share some of the things that I think should appear on one's agenda.

I realize I am being somewhat idealistic in making these suggestions. Some of those near death will lack either energy or cognitive ability to complete these tasks. Our individual circumstances may be different, and what each of us needs to do may be unique. I would not want anyone to feel guilty if he or she were not able to accomplish all of these things. Still, I urge my patients to think through their personal agendas and to use their final days and hours to do what is most crucial for them. Some readers may want to use my suggestions to make a checklist to ensure that they accomplish what is necessary, to be among those who finish life well.

I would also observe that though gradual death is on the increase, it is far from universal. Deaths tend to come in three different ways. First, death can approach gradually, pursuing a steady and relentless course. The time of death can be at least somewhat predictable. Many cancers and Lou Gehrig's disease (Amyotrophic Lateral Sclerosis), for example, cause this kind of death. It is important to understand that even these gradual deaths tend to occur more quickly than doctors and patients first expect. The fact is that most doctors predict that patients will have three to five times as many days till death than they actually experience.[2] Second, deaths can come suddenly, without warning. Third, deaths can come as the result of diseases that we can control for a long time with today's medicine but that will eventually be fatal. Albert was told eight years before his death that he had a very weak heart and that this condition would eventually take his life. He was an ideal patient and cooperated fully with his cardiologist. His deterioration was slow, and in spite of knowing how weak his heart was, everyone expected him to keep on going like the Energizer Bunny—until the day his wife found him collapsed in the bathroom. Dead! Albert knew death was coming but had no idea when. In that sense, even a gradual death can be sudden.

We can apply my suggested agenda most easily to the first scenario. The second scenario, however, presents more of a challenge. The possibility of sudden death makes it imperative that all of us work on completing the agenda now, so that if death were to overtake us unexpectedly, we would be prepared. The third scenario is equally difficult. I have learned that when the initial diagnosis is made, some careful thought should be given to the agenda we are about to discuss. Go ahead and have the serious talks about death and dying. But then it is okay to leave it there. There is no sense in focusing on your terminal diagnosis. Get out and live; enjoy each day knowing that whenever the end comes, you will be prepared.

An Agenda for Your Benefit
Review Your Life
Many people see the events of their lives from a new and fresh perspective when they view them in light of impending death. Dying people do not pretend to be something they are not. Masks come off; they are able to accept the good with the bad.[3] I encourage people to reflect on what they have accomplished for good, what they've failed to do, and where they've erred. Mature Christians will understand that all of the good things they have

done were accomplished by God's grace working in and through them. They will be able to confront their failures, confess what they did wrong, and repent of sin. Christians will not need to live in denial, even when the memories hurt, for they will find great comfort in realizing that by Christ's death they are forgiven. They will rejoice more in his forgiveness than be troubled by the sin, and they will find peace. Experiencing God's forgiveness, they will identify with the words of the converted slave trader, John Newton: "I am a great sinner and Christ is a great Saviour."[4] The result is that whether thinking about the good things or the sinful deeds of their lives, believers will have reason to give thanks and praise to God.

This life review also allows one to see that God used many of the difficulties of life to accomplish his purposes. None were wasted. This process will also encourage faith that the same God who has provided so well in the past will continue to provide till the end; it will bolster confidence in God.

Roland had suffered two strokes and was paralyzed on both sides. He was in a nursing home confined to bed. He did not like to watch TV and preferred not to leave his room. We talked about how he could make his days more pleasant. He asked his daughter to bring tag board to his room and plaster the wall with remembrances of God's blessing. He had his daughter attach the names and pictures of his family, some friends, his church, and a Bible—and one day I was honored to see my name there. As Roland reflected on his past blessings, he was constantly reminded that he had much to be thankful for.

Examine Your Faith

The apostle Paul exhorts us: "examine yourselves to see whether you are in the faith" (2 Cor. 13:5). Such self-inspection is never time wasted. Our Lord warns us that some will die and come into God's presence expecting to receive their eternal reward. They will cite numerous good things they have done in this life, thinking they have earned entrance into heaven. Tragically they will hear Jesus say, "I never knew you, depart from me . . ." (Matt. 7:23). If you have lived your life trying to please God and earn your way to heaven, now is the time to recognize that is impossible. Trust him. Find your rest and peace in what he has done.

Pray

Spending time in God's presence must be a high priority as life ends. Simply put, the more comfortable we are with God the easier it will be to go to him. Our prayers will likely take on a different emphasis. In our more active years we are tempted to focus on what we need or, even more, on what we want. Is it not wiser to focus our prayers on God and his glory? I find many of my older friends will pray this way. It is good to take time to meditate on the glorious character of God while reflecting on the wonders of creation and redemption. Be awed by the Holy Spirit. Allow God's love and presence to give you great joy and be deeply satisfied by him. One of the old saints prayed, "May the vision of your beauty be my death."[5] I would love to be so enamored with the beauty of God when I die that the very thrill causes my heart to stop and takes me into his presence. In addition to praying for God's glory we should spend more time giving thanks. Each day he grants us breath brings a series of blessings. Give thanks for life and for those who help you live it well. Most of all give thanks for the hope that you have of eternal life in him.

There will still be many needs around you that you should pray for. Pray for yourself. Pray for strength to die well. Pray that God will be glorified in your life till you breathe your last. In your prayers submit yourself to the will of God. It is appropriate for us to persevere in praying for healing but to do so with an attitude of submission to the will of God. Pray for others. At this time of your life you should appreciate what is truly important for your loved ones and family. Be praying that others will understand deep eternal truths. Pray for their character development and for their understanding of God and his ways. Take the words of Scripture and pray them into others' lives.

Last year I made a nursing home visit to a long-time friend who had been disabled by a devastating stroke. She was confined to bed and was growing progressively weaker. Her husband had recently died, and she spoke longingly of being with him in God's presence. She was having trouble sleeping and asked if I would give her something to help her sleep. I asked what her nights were like, and her response was, "Well, I just lie here most of the night praying." I asked what she was praying for, and she said, "I pray for my family, for the nurses, and every night I pray for you." I was tempted to say, "No way will I give you a sleeping pill!" But I realized I was being selfish and prescribed one. In a matter of weeks the Lord called her home.

Determine to Die Well

The end of life presents many uncertainties. The bottom line is that we neither know how nor when we will die. We might have understandable anxiety as we think about our future on earth. We need to share our anxiety with the Lord in prayer while at the same time telling him it is our intention to live our lives to the end for him. We must pray for the grace to die well.

Charlie had faithfully served as a church usher for over fifty years. Now he was dying of prostate cancer. He always said he had no pain, but you could tell he was minimizing his suffering. Nevertheless, he determined to be at the door of the church right to the end. He was doing what he felt God had called him to. He missed only three Sundays. Was Charlie being stubborn? You could say that. Did it help him die well? It surely did. Charlie kept going to the end because he made a mental commitment to die well.

We do not know what challenges lie ahead of us. However, as Christians we should not allow the unknown to be a stumbling block. If we know that Christ is with us, we can face the future with a bold confidence that he will give the strength we need when we need it.

An Agenda to Help Others

As we progress through these strategies, we see that finishing life well is not strictly about us and our comfort. We have already seen that it is about God and how we can glorify him. It is also about others. Our later days will have significant impact on the rest of the lives of those closest to us. If we use our later days well, we will aid their grieving. We will set a good example and help them know how to die when their turn comes.

Strengthen Family Relationships

Researchers report that 39 percent of terminally ill patients indicated that strengthening family bonds was one of their major priorities.[6] This is one of the unique opportunities afforded by a gradual death. I have often seen dysfunctional families start working well as a team when a loved one was approaching death. They would shed tears together, hug one another, and hold hands. They would forget bygone differences, and the family would connect in powerful ways.

Do not assume that family squabbles will be reconciled automatically. It may be necessary for the dying patient to directly confront family members. I can hear Fran take her two daughters aside and say, "Now Jill and Suzanne, isn't it time to forget what happened at Jimmy's wedding and start loving each other again?" The family may have been torn apart for years, but when Fran, on her deathbed, entreated her daughters in this way, Jill and Suzanne cried together, embraced and, let their quarrel go.

I often get into life and death discussions with families. People may disagree on how aggressive the medical care should be for an incapacitated parent. One child may push for surgery while another just wants comfort care. I will sometimes speak for the dying parent and say, "If your dad could get involved in this discussion, I suspect I know what he would say." Of course that triggers the question, "What do you think Dad would say?" I tell them that their parent would say, "You know, I don't really care what you decide. I know that my days are numbered and that whatever choice you make, I will likely die soon. What I do want is that after I am buried, my entire family continue to love each other." Once family members agree that this would be their parent's priority, the medical decision is often easier to make.

Stephen Kiernan writes:

> Yet many families are also discovering remarkable gifts in providing end of life care, an intimacy and richness without equal in their lives. . . . The shared courage and powerful bond between a person on life's last journey and family members easing that path can create nothing less than a new kind of love.[7]

Bequeath a Legacy

"Legacy" refers to anything handed down to a new generation from the past. This is what the psalmist David had in mind when he wrote:

> So even to old age and gray hairs,
>   O God, do not forsake me,
> until I proclaim your might to another generation,
>   your power to all those to come. (Ps. 71:18)

Christians have an opportunity to leave behind something more valuable and lasting than a piece of property or sum of money, as important as those might be. Just like David, we have the privilege of bequeathing to others a testimony to the might and power of God.

If we have reflected on the good and bad of our lives, now is the time to share some of that with those we will leave behind. One way to do this is by writing what I call "an autobiography of grace." Write your life story with God as the main character, not you. As you describe your experience of him and chronicle his gracious role in your life, you will be fulfilling Psalm 145:4: "One generation shall commend your works to another, and shall declare your mighty acts." This should be a worshipful experience for both you and those who read it. It may also be a way that your children and grandchildren will come to understand the faith you have embraced. Write about how God brought you to faith. Tell how he led you in marriage, career, and other life choices. Talk about his provision when you were struggling.

Some have chosen to write letters to their loved ones to be distributed after their deaths. I have heard of dying people writing letters to their children or grandchildren to be given to them at important life events like graduations or weddings.

How I wish I would have asked more about my ancestors. I was embarrassed when I was planning the memorial service for my father. I had to review with Mom the circumstances of his salvation. To this day I could not tell you anything about the spiritual pilgrimages of three of my four grandparents and very little about the other. I only know that they were believers and that they are now in the Lord's presence.

During their final days, many people try to meet with friends and relatives individually. There is great value in these one-on-one times. They may even do as Jacob did. Scripture tells how the patriarch met with and made some insightful comments to each of his sons and "blessed them." Who can fully appreciate the value of such a blessing from someone who truly cares about you? A dying person might want to think ahead of time about a message that would be meaningful to each one receiving it. The blessings might be nothing more than wishing them well or saying a final good-bye. "Good-bye," after all, is an abbreviation for "God Bless Ye." Since we don't know when any good-bye will be our last, we should not worry about saying it too soon. There is nothing wrong with pronouncing a final blessing long before we actually die. It's important that it is said sometime.

During these conversations it is good for the dying person to inquire how loved ones are coping with his or her dying. And loved ones need to be willing to share their feelings and talk openly with the terminally ill. I suggest to patients they simply say, "This illness of mine is forcing many changes in our family. How are you doing with it?" By carefully listening to loved ones' responses, the dying person may do much to help them cope with the impending death.

Have Some Enjoyable Time

I have seen dying patients having fun and not allowing grief to rob them of some good times as they near the end. This should be encouraged. As Christians our hope in God enables us to enjoy life to the end. I tell my patients: "It is okay to kick back, relax, and make the most of the days you have left. Watch some funny movies, have some good times laughing together with loved ones, and if your strength allows, do some things that you have always wanted to do." If you can travel to see old friends, spread a blessing as widely as you can. Paul Hiebert was a retired seminary professor who knew he was dying of cancer. He set out and visited as many friends and family as he could in his final months right up to near the time of his death. He was an inspiration to many. As much as you can, avoid always focusing on the fact that you are dying. After all, you are still living.

Provide Closure with Loved Ones

It is a blessing to have family and friends when you are terminally ill. I have attended terminally ill patients who had no one to be with them. Normally, dying people desire to spend time with loved ones and close friends. Do you remember Jeb who wanted the chocolate cake and coffee before he died? More than these treats he yearned for his family to be in the intensive care unit with him. One of the greatest gifts family can give to those who are dying is their presence; I never hear people express any regret over time spent with the dying.

Conversations between loved ones and the terminally ill will no doubt drift to serious matters. In his books *Dying Well* and *The Four Things That Matter Most*, Ira Byock tells how he encourages those coming to the end of life to say four things frequently:

1. I love you.
2. Thank you.

3. Forgive me.
4. I forgive you.[8]

Simply saying these four things, Byock says, brings people to a sense of completion and a state of tranquility. As a Christian, impressed with this wisdom, I have come to realize how much Jesus would have encouraged us to say these same things.

Those near death will need to think about their relationships, asking who it is that needs to hear these words. It's too easy to assume that certain people know that these things are true, though we may never have clearly said them. We might need to look back many years. We might find some damaged relationships that have never been repaired. Even those the dying person sees every day may still need to hear these four expressions. The apostle Paul tells us: "If possible, so far as it depends on you, live peaceably with all" (Rom. 12:18). As the days of life come to an end, we should be particularly concerned that we are at peace with all.

Whom do we truly love but have failed to tell in words that they will remember? Many fathers assume that because they give their children gifts to show their love, they do not need to verbalize it. What these dads do not realize is how much those children are waiting to hear them say, "I love you." After their father is gone, the children will remember those words much more than they will remember the gifts. Our love must be seen in our actions, but it must also be spoken. Unfortunately, I have never been quick to tell anyone I loved them. My two sons often end our phone conversations with "I love you." That has helped me learn to say those words more frequently.

We are quick to accept favors from others, and, all too often, we take them for granted. Those we love need to know that we appreciate the things they do for us. We must take time to talk about the many kindnesses we have received from them and let them know that we appreciate them. Scripture repeatedly teaches us to be thankful. Say "thank you" often.

Many relationships are fragmented because one or both parties are unwilling to admit that they were wrong. Scripture admonishes us to confess our sins to each other. That involves seeking forgiveness for the wrong things we have done. All of us have close relationships where we have been guilty of some wrongdoing. We may not see it as anything significant. However, the one who suffered the injustice may not view it with similar disregard. We must be willing to say "forgive me" frequently.

The other side of the coin can be equally destructive. When we hold a grudge and refuse to forgive others, we may keep them from the joy and fullness in life that they could otherwise have. In that case we hold them in bondage by our refusal to forgive. If we do not forgive them now (and tell them so), we will die having not taken advantage of the opportunity God gives us. Recall how Jesus condemned the servant who had been forgiven much but was unwilling to forgive little (Matt. 18:21–35). If we have found God's forgiveness, surely we will forgive those who have wronged us. Forgiving another is not simply about dying with a clear conscience. It is much more about enabling the one you are forgiving to live well. Forgiveness is a precious gift that you can give before you die. Do not hesitate to say, "I forgive you."

Not only must the dying person say these four things, they must hear them as well. Initiating these conversations may help bring closure to many of your earthly relationships. That is an essential part of dying well. But do not wait too long to talk to loved ones; you might lose the opportunity. Joe is a tragic story of one who did not say and hear the four things soon enough.

A likeable guy, Joe was fun to be around. He always had an eye for people who needed help and was right there for them. He and his wife, Shirley, loved their children and grandchildren and could talk incessantly about them. Joe had just retired and was looking forward to days with his family, time on the golf course, and more time to simply enjoy life. I knew Joe well, and always looked forward to his coming to the office.

All was not rosy, though. Joe had a son, Frank, whom I had never met, one who was considered the black sheep of the family. Though there was no open animosity, Joe and Frank did not have much of a relationship. In fact, they had not talked for several years. It bothered Joe a lot. He wanted to reach out to his son, but his efforts had been rebuffed before and now he was uncharacteristically afraid. Joe spent a lot of time thinking about Frank and his family.

The other problem Joe faced was that he had been a heavy drinker for the first half of his adult life. He had developed cirrhosis of the liver and as a result had had several stomach hemorrhages. One Wednesday morning he arrived unscheduled at the office to report he had been vomiting blood for over forty-five minutes. He was immediately admitted to intensive care and started on medications to control the stomach bleeding. After receiving several pints of blood, Joe felt somewhat better, but he continued to ooze blood from his stomach. Suddenly Friday afternoon he had severe pain in the right side of his chest and he could hardly breathe. He was turning blue and was in severe distress. An immediate CAT scan confirmed the suspicion that Joe had developed a pulmonary embolus—blood clots in his lungs. Everyone knew that the combination of blood clots and hemorrhage could be fatal.

During the night Joe's breathing became more shallow, and he struggled for each breath. Joe was placed on a breathing machine to provide the sorely needed oxygen he could not get any other way. His family was called and were there when I arrived shortly after. All but Frank. Joe was awake but could not talk because of the tube in his mouth. He was fully aware that he had almost died and that his life was now being preserved by the machine breathing for him. He was able to write notes and made it clear that he wanted Frank there. Joe wanted to tell Frank he loved him. He longed to tell him he forgave him for walking out of his life and to ask Frank to forgive him for the way he had treated him in the past.

Shirley was able to contact Frank and explain the dire situation Joe was in. To her great relief, Frank said that he would come when he could, hoping to do so within a week. The whole family was pleased, though frustrated with the delay. Joe wrote me a note saying that he knew that he may not survive, but was there any way we could keep him alive until Frank arrived? I assured him we would do what we could.

Frank called and said that he had gotten on a flight and would arrive in eight hours. Joe was trying to hang on. It was about six hours later that Joe's heart stopped; he was in cardiac arrest. In spite of doing everything possible, we could not keep him going. Joe died without ever seeing Frank. Frank arrived thirty minutes later. Shirley was waiting for him outside the ICU. When he arrived, they hugged, and Shirley told Frank that Joe had desperately tried to hang on to see him but did not make it. Now he was dead. They went together arm in arm to see the body. Frank could not hold it together. Sobbing, he kissed his father's forehead. It was too late. Joe could not respond.

Joe died before he could finish his life's work. He had a longing that was never filled. Shirley looks back on his death with frustration. Frank has not been able to forgive himself for not coming sooner. Simply put, Joe did not die well. If only Joe had known earlier that his life was ending.

Once we are dead and gone, we will leave few things behind. One lasting memorial will be our loving families and good relationships. Saying and hearing these four things will help ensure that.

Conclusion

If we recognize that we are slowly dying, we have a window of opportunity to make the best of the waning days of our lives. We will no longer be worried about how we will die or even when. We can simply accept it and determine to live each day well so that when the time comes, we will be ready. We should desire to make the most of each day. Because we do not know when death will come, each of us should be working on our agenda today. I encourage you to examine your faith, pray, and make sure that you have good relationships with your family and loved ones *today*. Begin to think through what legacy you will leave. But in the process don't forget to have fun. And say the four things frequently.

Prayer

Heavenly Father, my times are in your hands. I want them there. I do not know when death will come to me, but Father, when it does I want to die well. I want to leave this earth a better place. Please help me to leave my family stronger. Guide me by your Spirit to complete the agenda that you would have for me.

MEDITATION

O Jesus, I have promised
To serve thee to the end;
Be thou forever near me,
My Master and my Friend;
I shall not fear the battle
If thou art by my side,
Nor wander from the pathway
If thou wilt be my Guide.

O, let me hear thee speaking,
In accents clear and still,
Above the storms of passion,
The murmurs of self-will;
O, speak to reassure me,
To hasten, or control;
O, speak, and make me listen,
Thou Guardian of my soul.

O, let me see thy footmarks,
And in them plant mine own;
My hope to follow duly
Is in thy strength alone.

O, guide me, call me, draw me,
Uphold me to the end;
And then to rest receive me,
My Savior and my Friend.

"O JESUS, I HAVE PROMISED,"
JOHN BODE (1868)

Make Appropriate Use of Technology

What is a biblical understanding of technology?

How can technology help us?

What are the dangers of technology?

How do I use technology wisely?

M y friend Lee is a prime example of how one can benefit from modern medical technology. At age seventy he is actively using his skills as an electrician to serve many churches and Christian groups. He is able to do that because thirty years ago, when he was first diagnosed with coronary disease, he had a bypass that kept his heart going. Then ten years later, when he ruptured what would have otherwise been a fatal aortic aneurysm, he had emergency surgery to repair the tear, enabling him to survive with an excellent quality of life. Ten years after that his heart condition required another bypass. Since then Lee has been on potent drugs to reduce his cholesterol, and has had no further crises. His life of service today is testimony to the gift God has given us of life-saving technology; for these things we should be eternally grateful.

On the other hand technology is not always a blessing. At age ninety-two Tom lived independently without any family members nearby. His major social connections were within his church where he had been involved for decades. One Sunday, just before Christmas, he casually mentioned to his pastor that when the time came to die, he wanted to do it at church. Several weeks later, while in the sanctuary listening to the choir practicing, he had a cardiac arrest and collapsed into the aisle. A 911 call brought paramedics who quickly shocked and restarted his heart. He was transported to a nearby hospital emergency room. The emergency room physician greeted me with the words: "John, we have a save." But, a "save" it was not; when I evaluated Tom, there was little sign of any brain activity even though he was clearly not brain dead. After a week in the intensive care unit on maximal life support, he died. This was not the death Tom would have chosen for himself. Many would say Tom's final week was evidence of technology gone awry.

Technology is an unavoidable part of our lives. Very few of us will die without having to make some difficult decisions as to how much medical care we should seek to prolong our lives. The medical options we have available did not exist one hundred years ago, and many were unheard of just a few decades ago. Now they are increasing at an exponential pace. Options such as resuscitation, use of a breathing machine, open heart surgery, chemotherapy, or even whether to take penicillin for a strep throat all represent potentially life-extending choices we may have to make. Many of these alternatives can significantly lengthen and improve the quality of our lives. If we are viewing death as an enemy to be defeated, we will want all possible treatments. We should thank God for them and pursue life aggressively. But if death is near and treatment options less attractive, we will view death as a defeated enemy and choose not to use technology that will make our dying a fight to the bitter end. Thirty-five years ago I heard it said that we have much more *knowledge* about how to prolong life than *wisdom* concerning when to prolong it. If that was the situation then, it is much more the case today.

That brings us to our next strategy for coming to the end of life well: strategy 7: Make Appropriate Use of Technology. In this chapter, I recommend a balanced approach to utilizing medical technology, one that aims at defeating disease when possible while at the same time recognizing that we cannot ultimately escape death.

There is no question that technology can do many positive things, but it also presents problems. Seventeenth-century French mathematician and philosopher Blaise Pascal wrote:

> As men are not able to fight against death, misery, ignorance, they have taken it into their heads, in order to be happy, not to think of them at all. . . . We run carelessly to the precipice, after we have put something before us to prevent us seeing it.[1]

My fellow geriatrician, Pete Jaggard, comments that aggressive medical care can keep us from seeing the precipice we are running toward. He calls it the "Pascalian diversion."[2] Fighting death can be all-consuming. In the previous strategy we discussed many things we need to do if we are to come to the end of life well. All too often, intensive care, life support, surgery, and other life-saving efforts don't prevent patients from dying, but they do prevent them from attending to the agenda that will enable them to die well. Furthermore they contribute to the myth that death will not inevitably come.

A Biblical View of Technology
God Has Given Dominion
Recall the mandate God gave humanity immediately after creating the world:

Then God said, "Let us make man in our image, after our likeness. And let them have dominion over the fish of the sea and over the birds of the heavens and over the livestock and over all the earth and over every creeping thing that creeps on the earth. (Gen. 1:26)

Over the centuries, this God-given dominion has led to the invention of all sorts of technology. Today, our lives are largely dependent on these advances; most of them are good things for which we should thank God. Let there be no question that God can use technology to undo the results of sin. When there is a positive response to any treatment, we should give due credit to those who invent and are able to use the technology, but ultimately we should bow in thanksgiving to God for giving the brains and the ability.

God Wants Many to Be Healed

God may intend that some diseases lead to death, but in many situations he accomplishes his glory by defeating disease. Jesus did this by healing vast numbers of sick people. God continues to heal today principally in two ways. He works through people trained in the number of healing arts, and he works through prayer.[3]

God Works through Us

Repeatedly we see in Scripture how God works though humans. Even when performing a miracle, he often chooses to use the contributions of people. Jesus did this when he fed a group that included five thousand hungry men sitting on a hillside listening to him teach. Recognizing their need, he decided to meet it. He could have prayed, and God would have raised their blood sugars fifty points. Or he could have asked the Father to fill their bellies with roast beef and mashed potatoes. He chose instead to use what a little boy had to offer: five loaves and two fish. It wasn't much, but in the Lord's hands it was enough to feed the multitude. I often consider the medications that I prescribe as nothing more than five loaves and two fish. I will sometimes encourage my patients to bow and thank God for their medication before they take it, asking him to "bless it to their body's use." I do not believe that the drugs fundamentally do anything without God's help. The old adage, "God heals, the physician accepts the fee" is quite true.

Prayer Can Empower Technology

All too often I get things in the wrong order. I try to prescribe the best treatment for patients, and then if it does not work I ask if I might pray with them. Ideally, we should pray first. I love to have patients come to me and say, "John, I have been praying that you would come up with the right diagnosis and treatment for me." James stresses the role of prayer in treating illness: "Is anyone among you sick? Let him call for the elders of the church, and let them pray over him, anointing him with oil in the name of the Lord. And the prayer of faith will save the one who is sick, and the Lord will raise him up . . ." (James 5:14–15). The significance of oil in this passage is not clear. It may represent the Holy Spirit, used as a symbol of his work. It may represent a healing therapy used in that day and therefore be the equivalent of our technology. The intention is clear that whatever else we do, we should pray for healing—of the soul as well as the body. If we want someone to be healed, we should simply state our desire; but our prayers should not be in the form of a demand but rather as a request to our loving father. Out of respect for his greater wisdom we qualify our request in the way Jesus prayed: "Nevertheless, not my will, but yours, be done" (Luke 22:42). Furthermore Paul teaches us that there is a time to stop praying as he himself did about his "thorn in the flesh": "Three times I pleaded with the Lord about this, that it should leave me. But he said to me, 'My grace is sufficient for you, for my power is made perfect in weakness'" (2 Cor. 12:8–9).

Technology Can Be Bad

Technology Can Become a God. It is possible to make a god of the science of medicine. Viewing the medical profession as all-knowing and all-wise can turn the practice of medicine into a religious cult. The physicians become the priests we rely on for healing. I am at times disturbed when even Christian patients seem to have more confidence in their doctors than in the Lord. In this way, we can turn medical technology into an idol to be worshiped.

Reject the "Technologic Imperative." Some philosophers of science write of what they term "the technologic imperative."[4] This is the belief that technological progress must be pursued regardless of the cost. It implies that if something *can* be done, it *must* be done. Christians should flatly reject this thinking, because it may result in all sorts of morally unacceptable practices. Yet I find that it is all too common for Christians to succumb to the technologic imperative.

Jack had extensive surgery to treat his pancreatic cancer nine months before he died from the disease. But within six months of the surgery, it became clear that the entire cancer had not been removed. He then received two different chemotherapy agents, which were not effective. Hearing of a possible cure offered by a cancer clinic in another state, he concluded he had nothing to lose by "giving it a try." But this promised cure didn't even relieve his pain. Jack died four weeks later, having been kept alive on a breathing and kidney machine for the last two weeks of his life. He was cut off from most of his family and loved ones, and they felt there had been no closure to his life. In the end he had regretted his decisions. While not being critical of what Jack chose to do, we recognize that just because something might be possible doesn't make it wise. In one sense we admire his spirit; in another sense, we must ask if he succumbed to the technologic imperative. When Christians choose treatments with a high likelihood of major side effects and a low chance of success, I often wonder, "Is heaven really so bad that we have to fight so hard to keep out?"

More Technology Does Not Equate to Love and Honor. Because seeing parents or loved ones die is always difficult, we naturally tend to want to hold on to them and approve any technology that will keep them alive. It is tough to draw the line and say, "That's enough aggressive treatment; just let her go." I have frequently seen children push for life-prolonging measures that go beyond what is reasonable or what they would even want for themselves. It seems that for many people their refusal to "let go" and their push for life-sustaining treatment is symbolic of love and commitment.[5] The logic goes somewhat like this: "I love my mother, I do not want her to die, and therefore I want to keep her alive as long as possible." Nursing home chaplain Hank Dunn has observed that this thinking is rarely based on medical or ethical reasons but rather on an emotional unwillingness to let go.[6] The fallacy of this thinking is that the life-prolonging measures are often very uncomfortable for the patient, rarely lead to prolonged quality living, and frequently prolong suffering. This failure to let go may be neither loving nor honoring to the parent. It may not be what the parent herself would have wanted. I have learned long ago never to ask children, "Now what would you like us to do for your Mom?" No, the proper question is, "If Mom were able to speak for herself, what would she want us to do in this situation?"

Technology Is Costly. Besides causing unnecessary suffering, life-prolonging measures result in unnecessary spending. They are part of the reason that over 27 percent of Medicare expenditures are spent in the last twelve months of life.[7] I was talking to a missionary nurse once about these concerns, and she said simply, "Stop doing this and we could vaccinate all of the children in the world; it would be a far better investment."

There Will Always Be Some Risk. Before agreeing to a medical procedure, I urge those making the decisions to consider the risks involved—and believe me, there are always risks. One of my partners is well known for saying, "Medicines are poisons that have some good side effects!" I often tell students, "Once you understand the patient's problem, your first question must be, what am I prescribing that is causing it?"

Mike was a godly man in his early seventies. He was active in his church and frequently visited homebound patients. He seemed to be in excellent health. One Monday morning I was paged to the emergency room, where Mike was having a heart attack. He had excruciating pressure on his chest, his lungs were filling with fluid, and he was becoming more confused as his blood pressure dropped. In short he was dying. Without some intervention he would not live out the morning. This occurred some years ago, when physicians routinely administered clot-dissolving medications in cases like Mike's. I initiated that treatment, and within thirty minutes things were going much better. It was like a miracle; Mike's pain was gone, his blood pressure was up, and he was breathing and thinking normally. I was thrilled and, along with his wife, praised God for the gift of those medications. However, at two o'clock that afternoon I received word that Mike's speech was slurred and that he was paralyzed on the right side. An emergency CAT scan revealed that Mike had a brain hemorrhage, no doubt caused by the "miracle drug." I knew immediately the hemorrhage would be fatal; he died three days later. A hemorrhage like that happens in 2 percent of cases, but for Mike it was 100 percent. Such a risk is clearly justified in a case like Mike's, because he was dying anyway. But what about the person who dies from a complication of a plastic surgery procedure for a condition that is not life threatening? While it is easy to get excited about the amazing things that medical science can do, it is important to recognize that there are risks as well.

We cannot assume, even in the most straightforward case, that the outcome of a medical treatment will be good. Nor can we assume in the most complicated high-risk situation, that the outcome will be bad. The challenge is to make the best decision we can in the face of uncertainty. My sons both took a course in college titled "Optimization in the Face of Uncertainty." Whereas I would never have understood the higher mathematics taught in the course, I understand the difficulty of making treatment decisions when there is so much uncertainty.

Guiding Principles for the Use of Technology
Several basic principles are worth considering as we reflect on our use of technology.

Be Aggressive Early

Medical treatment is usually most helpful when used early in the course of a disease. When used later, the results are much less impressive. For example, chemotherapy can cure many cancers when they are caught early, but late in the course of the disease chemotherapy's effectiveness is limited. Delayed treatment may add a few weeks or months to one's life, but it is often at the expense of much pain and suffering. Frequently too much treatment near the end of life actually speeds up the dying process. Even when it is probable that it will add some time to one's life, we must ask whether those additional days will be worth the pain and trauma the treatment itself can cause. It's important that we not procrastinate out of fear or uncertainty or some other reason; we should pursue diagnosis and treatment early when we are faced with a disease.

Define Your Purpose Clearly

Too often various technologies are used near the end of life without a clear understanding of one's goal. Hank Dunn advises us to be very clear concerning the purpose of treatment and to be ready to reevaluate it. He suggests three possible goals for treatment:

1. Cure
2. Stabilize function
3. Prepare for a comfortable and dignified death[8]

If there is a good possibility of restoring health, we should probably use all means available to do so. On the other hand if we are merely seeking to stabilize a person's condition and, even more, if we are preparing someone for a comfortable and dignified death, we should limit the steps we are willing to take. Further, we must be ready to reevaluate these goals as time goes on. For example, if you had pneumonia, you would take an antibiotic intended to cure—which it often does. However, in the course of that treatment it is possible to develop respiratory failure, when the lungs can no longer provide sufficient oxygen. If this were to happen to you, you would need a breathing machine, called a ventilator, for several days till the lungs began to recover. In this case it would be fine to use the ventilator. There would be every reason to expect full recovery. The goal of the antibiotic and of the breathing machine would be cure. But sometimes, particularly when there is underlying chronic lung disease, a patient may not be able to get off the ventilator. That which was intended to cure would now simply prolong life. At that point it would be wise to reevaluate the situation and ask anew what one's goal is and should one still be using the ventilator.

Unfortunately there is not always a clear distinction between treatments designed to cure and those used for giving comfort. The latter will at times unavoidably prolong life. This creates difficulties for those who want their symptoms to be treated but not at the expense of senselessly prolonging life. This was Harry's situation. Dying of congestive heart failure, he had no interest in continuing to live. Though he had been given near maximal treatment, his heart was steadily deteriorating. I explained to him the dilemma facing us: if we used any medication to cope with his physical distress, it would also likely keep him alive longer. I gently encouraged him to take medications that would ease his distress, enroll in hospice, and allow the caregivers to make his last days easier. He kept asking if doing so would make him live longer; when I told him it would, he repeatedly refused all help. He chose instead to return home, where he died several days later—but only after long hours of agony as his lungs filled with fluid.

There Is No Moral Difference between Withholding and Withdrawing Care

We must ask the following important question: "Is there any moral difference between withholding care and withdrawing it?" For instance, one patient might make the decision not to treat his life-threatening cancer with chemotherapy; another patient (or patient's family) might decide to stop a treatment that has been keeping him alive. Most bioethicists, Christian or not, will say that there is no distinction. Either withdrawing or withholding may be right in one situation, and either may be wrong in another.

A common struggle in intensive care units involves the care of a patient with near end-stage emphysema. If the lungs fail, a ventilator is necessary to sustain life. But it is never certain that a patient will be able to get off the machine and return to breathing on his own. There is always a chance that he will become permanently dependent on the ventilator. Many would not choose to be kept alive that way. In some ways it is easier if the physician does not prescribe this treatment—in other words, withholds care. But that might hinder some possibility of life. The other option is to use the machine with a time limit in mind. For example, family members and doctors might decide to use the ventilator for up to five days, but if the patient is unable to breathe on his own by the end of that time, the treatment would be stopped. This would amount to withdrawing care. Making such a decision can be excruciatingly difficult for loved ones. Yet taking a patient off of a ventilator can be done humanely by using appropriate doses of morphine to deal with the resulting shortness of breath. In addition to being a painkiller, morphine decreases the body's drive to breathe. If someone is struggling for air, a small dose of morphine can make her quite comfortable. Once the drug is administered, the breathing machine can be turned off without causing great distress. At times patients never breathe on their own, and die quickly. More commonly they will breathe for several hours, and die slowly. Some who were not given much hope of recovery will actually do quite well. A time-limited trial keeps the survivors from saying, "We never even tried."

Leona is eighty-six and has severe emphysema. She uses oxygen around-the-clock and has been in the hospital five times in the last two years. Each admission has been precipitated by worsening of her lung disease and has kept her in the hospital for about a week. On two occasions she required a ventilator to keep her alive. The first time it was for one day, but at the last admission she was on the machine for three days. She hated those experiences and made it clear that she did not want to have a machine keep her alive. Her doctor suggested that she put a time limit on the treatment, and it is now understood that if Leona is ever in the situation where she cannot get off the ventilator in seven days, her doctor will sedate her with appropriate doses of morphine and remove the machine. She knows that such an action might lead to death, but she also knows that a ventilator might save her life.

Weigh the Burden against the Potential Benefit

When we are pondering whether to use certain technologies, it is helpful to picture a scale in our minds with the potential benefits in one tray and the potential burdens in the other. The burdens we need to consider include such things as the financial, emotional, and physical (in terms of pain and suffering) costs as well as the risks involved. We must then ask, "Which way does the scale tip?" This type of analysis is nothing more than what Jesus taught when he said, "first sit down and count the cost . . ." (Luke 14:28).

In my experience as a geriatrician, this cost counting is crucial when treating an elderly person who is acutely ill. It is well known that the elderly are more prone to develop complications from any treatment, whether it is a simple pill or major surgery. We do one thing and it hurts something else; we seek to help one complication and we get another. It is often for this reason that we find ourselves dealing with a cascade of problems and frequently get into a level of intervention that we never anticipated when we first embarked on doing something "simple."

At ninety-two Marge was becoming increasingly disabled by the osteoarthritis of her knees. She elected to have her left knee replaced. The surgery went well. But after surgery, even though appropriate measures were taken to prevent them, blood clots developed in her legs and were not recognized till they had traveled to her lungs. She became so short of breath that she was moved to the intensive care unit and placed on a ventilator. It was only after a month in intensive care and another three weeks in the hospital that she was moved to a nursing home. Needless to say she was not happy with the result. Had she understood the burdens of her knee replacement, I suspect she would have elected to forgo the surgery and live with the bad knee.

Is It Considered Ordinary or Extraordinary Care?

Ordinary care is the minimal level of care that we all deserve as human beings made in the image of God; it includes such things as being given food to eat and fluids to drink, being kept warm, and receiving loving compassion. It is what Jesus refers to in the following passage:

> Then the King will say to those on his right, "Come, you who are blessed by my Father, inherit the kingdom prepared for you from the foundation of the world. For I was hungry and you gave me food, I was thirsty and you gave me drink, I was a stranger and you welcomed me, I was naked and you clothed me, I was sick and you visited me, I was in prison and you came to me." Then the righteous will answer him, saying, "Lord, when did we see you hungry and feed you, or thirsty and give you drink? And when did we see you a stranger and welcome you, or naked and clothe you? And when did we see you sick or in prison and visit you?" And the King will answer them, "Truly, I say to you, as you did it to one of the least of these my brothers, you did it to me." (Matt. 25:34–40)

Because there are so many technological options open to us, our challenge is to define what is ordinary versus extraordinary care. I consider extraordinary care to be anything that involves potentially life-prolonging treatment; we are not required to pursue such care. My good friend Dr. Ben Mitchell suggests that extraordinary care is anything that involves plastic tubing. I have wondered if it might include anything that was not available to Jesus in his day. The use of any technology must be considered according to context, and we must never assume it is morally necessary. Extraordinary care may be wrong in the following contexts:

1. It violates the expressed wishes of the patient.
2. It is generally felt to be futile.

3. It is presented as being more effective or less risky than it truly is.
4. It is an effort to defy God's will that the patient die.

It is wrong to forgo extraordinary care in the following contexts:

1. In the values of the patient the benefits outweigh the burdens.
2. It is expected to restore the patient to a reasonable level of function.
3. The desire to do so is driven by an irrational fear of suffering or losing control.
4. The choice is mandated by finances or outside authority whose primary motivation is not the patient's well-being.

Perhaps a better way to deal with the issues related to providing extraordinary versus ordinary care is one Pope John Paul II proposed in 1980. He suggested we think in terms of proportionate vs. disproportionate care. I feel this is a more useful distinction, because it places the emphasis more on the context than on the technology. For example, treating pneumonia with an antibiotic and possibly a ventilator in an intensive care unit may be considered extraordinary care in any context. However, treating a healthy fifty-year-old for pneumonia would surely be proportionate while treating a ninety-eight-year-old dying of metastatic cancer in the same way may be disproportionate. The morality of these treatments is not a question of the technology but rather of the context.

When do we intervene and use technology to treat a serious medical condition, and when do we sit back and say we will let the patient die naturally? This is, of course, the tough question. God always knows what is right or wrong for us, and there are right and wrong answers to each dilemma we face. Paul makes the point in Romans 8 that while we are not under the law (meaning the Law of Moses), we are under what he refers to as, "the law of the Spirit of life" (Rom. 8:2). God as the Holy Spirit resides in us and he will prompt us to know what is right. We must seek his direction in every situation of life and then obey it.

Appendix 2 looks at specific technologies available to prolong life.

Conclusion

We have come closer to understanding how the proper use of technology may fit into God's plans at the end of life. I know that I want to come to the end of life when God calls me home, not when technology fails. To do that will likely require that at some time I will say no to some available technology and pursue comfort care, which I discuss in strategy 8.

Prayer

Father, I am so thankful to live in the era of modern medicine. You have given us so many ways to relieve suffering and to increase our productive life span. But Lord, these issues are so complex. I want to live a full life to honor you, but I do not want to use excessive technology to resist you when you call me home. Grant me the wisdom to know how to respond when the questions arise. I desire that you will be glorified by my choices.

═══════════ Meditation ═══════════

O Lord, our Lord,
   how majestic is your name in all the earth!
You have set your glory above the heavens.
   Out of the mouth of babies and infants,
you have established strength because of your foes,
   to still the enemy and the avenger.

When I look at your heavens, the work of your fingers,
   the moon and the stars, which you have set in place,

what is man that you are mindful of him,
    and the son of man that you care for him?

Yet you have made him a little lower than the heavenly
        beings
    and crowned him with glory and honor.
You have given him dominion over the works of your
        hands;
    you have put all things under his feet,
all sheep and oxen,
    and also the beasts of the field,
the birds of the heavens, and the fish of the sea,
    whatever passes along the paths of the seas.

O LORD, our Lord,
    how majestic is your name in all the earth!

PSALM 8

Changing Gears from Cure to Comfort Care

What does it mean to change from cure to comfort care?

Why do we make the change?

When do we make the change?

How do we make the change?

Remember Jeb? He was the man who asked for chocolate cake and coffee as he was coming to the end of life. I have told his story frequently over the years. Almost to the person, everyone smiles and nods their head, communicating to me, "When my time comes I want to go like that." But that type of death does not happen automatically. It didn't for Jeb. He made purposeful choices and was careful to communicate his wishes clearly. You see, one day several months before he died, Jeb came to my office with his daughter to discuss end-of-life issues, and he made it clear that he did not want to pursue any heroics. If he were to have another heart attack, he wanted to be made comfortable but did not want resuscitation or other life-sustaining treatment. Thus, when the time came to face the difficult decisions of life support or other treatment, Jeb, his family, and I were all prepared.

My experience with Leo was a totally different story. He was a middle-aged man who never suspected that he had a terminal disease. Yet, when I diagnosed his illness as pancreatic cancer, his malignancy had already spread through his body. He made it very clear that his goal was to beat the cancer; he was determined not to give in to it. His wife continually reinforced that mindset to those of us who were caring for him. She would repeatedly implore Leo not to give up. In spite of his unfailing spirit, he continued to deteriorate and went from one complication to another. I talked to Leo about when it would be appropriate to change from pressing for the cure (which was not going to happen) to pursuing comfort care. Leo said that when the time came, he wanted to die at home, but he was not willing to "give up" just then. He continued to ask for aggressive treatment. When he was no longer able to breathe on his own, he was kept alive by a ventilator. Within several days he became paralyzed below his neck, the cancer having damaged his spinal cord. Even after he lapsed into a coma, his wife reminded us that Leo's last wish was that everything be done to keep him alive. Leo lived for another three weeks dependent on the ventilator, while the cancer continued to ravage his body. All organs eventually shut down. Leo died in the intensive care unit, never having the opportunity to have a time of closure with his family. He did not get his wish to die at home.

Both Jeb and Leo were near the end of their lives. But their deaths were radically different—a difference resulting from the choices they had made. I suspect that most would agree that Jeb made the wiser choices. When in a situation like Jeb's and Leo's, you can legitimately make choices that will affect how and when you die. Most often, the choice involves choosing between quality of life and the hope for a little longer life. The question often comes down to: "Do we use technology to seek to get a little more time before death comes, or do we resign ourselves to the fact that death is inevitable and stop seeking to resist it?" If you know that death is coming soon, it may not be worth struggling to live a few more days. Quality of life may be much more important than quantity. You acknowledge that you are dying; it is not a question of if, but how and when. At that point it may no longer be appropriate to fight, but to come to peace with the inevitable and prepare for it. Then it is time to implement strategy 8: Changing Gears from Cure to Comfort Care. This is when we change the goal of our medical care from that which is intent on finding a cure to that which is designed to minimize symptoms and provide comfort. It is not necessarily an all-or-nothing decision. We may choose against technology with major burden and little benefit, but still want some life-sustaining treatment that has little burden but much benefit.

If we do not change gears, we will continue to choose every treatment option available until each one fails. Typically we will come to the end of life in an intensive care unit after repeated attempts at resuscitation. It will be true that we will have fought valiantly to preserve life and resist death, the great enemy. This is what poet Dylan Thomas advised:

> Do not go gentle into that good night,
> Old age should burn and rave at close of day;
> Rage, rage against the dying of the light.[1]

But is this what we want? If not, we will have to choose to change gears before we get to this point. In this chapter we will consider why, when, and how we may choose to limit technology that will only delay an inevitable death.

Why Change Gears?
Changing Gears Allows You to Prepare
Changing gears confirms that you have a clear understanding that death is coming. There is no denying it. That opens up opportu-

nities to prepare for death. The psalmist asked that God would teach us to number our days so that we could live wisely (Ps. 90:12). The implication is that realizing you are going to die allows you an entirely new and wiser perspective on life. The Puritans lived with a constant awareness of death. The children in the family of eighteenth-century Jonathan Edwards wrote over and over in their copybooks, "Nothing is more certain than death. Take no delay in the great work of preparing for death."[2] If you are using all technology possible to forestall death, if you are hoping against hope that you will be the one to beat the odds, chances are you will not take the time to prepare to die. You will not seek out time with your family to bring closure to your life, and death will sneak up on you.

Changing gears will give you great freedom to openly discuss death with your loved ones. They will know that you have accepted it, and that will likely help them to accept that you are dying. I have seen how changing gears can make the final days on earth very rich. It enables you to concentrate on your last days, not on all of the things involved in pointless treatment. It allows you to say the four things (I love you, thank you, forgive me, and I forgive you) and accomplish the other agenda we discussed in chapter 6. In these ways changing gears may exchange quantity of days for quality of life. We don't change gears and opt for quality of life simply to avoid pain and suffering but rather to preserve for us the potential to use our last days well, often focused on others. This approach to the end of life can allow God to be glorified in greater ways than if we struggle to delay death a little longer.

Changing Gears Allows You and Others to Focus on Comfort Care
Making a decision to no longer prolong your life can significantly reduce your suffering because your doctor can be free to order stronger pain relievers than would otherwise be appropriate. You may decide to forgo painful tests or surgeries.

I remember Sal, who had terminal ovarian cancer. She was unable to make the decision to change gears though I had encouraged her to do so. One Monday morning her daughter called me and said that Sal was in horrible pain and had not slept all night. I told the daughter to immediately call 911 and that I would meet her at the hospital. This she did, and her mother arrived in the emergency room about ten minutes before I did. By the time I got to her, those attending her had started an IV, drawn blood, and sent her off for a CAT scan. I was incensed, because she was still writhing in pain. I ordered morphine immediately. Had Sal made the decision to change gears and had she made it known that she was not seeking life-prolonging treatment, her needs would have been attended to much sooner.

There are many such occasions when seeking to prolong life will prevent truly compassionate care. Many voices urge comfort care, including the late Pope John Paul II:

> Those engaged in health care should certainly omit no effort in applying the full skills of their art to the advantage of the sick and dying. They should also bear in mind, however, that there is another consolation such people need and need even more urgently: unlimited kindness and devoted charity. When service of this kind is rendered to human beings, it is also rendered to Christ himself, who said: "as often as you did it for one of my least brothers, you did it for me."[3]

What the late pope is urging can be done in the context of aggressive care as well as comfort care, but it seems it is more likely in the context of the latter. Christian ethicist, John Kilner, writes, "If we reach a point at which we are no longer able to cope with suffering, if it overwhelms our capacity to experience God's goodness, then it loses its value and becomes merely destructive."[4] His point is that when suffering becomes overwhelming, it is appropriate to seek symptom-limiting care.

MOST PEOPLE DO NOT WANT LIFE-SUSTAINING TREATMENT AT THE END

One indication of the benefits of changing gears is that so many people are choosing to do so. I have been impressed over the years, particularly by my elderly patients, how ambivalent the older generation is about life-prolonging treatment. These patients often view it as simply death-delaying. Frequently, if they *do* consent to treatment, it is not because they want it, but because they do not want to disappoint their children who are not emotionally prepared to let go.

Shortly after the death of his beloved Ruth, Billy Graham was interviewed by *Time* magazine. They asked if, with all of our advanced medical technology, we perhaps fear death and fight it too much. Billy responded, "I think we often do, I'm convinced that in some cases we aren't so much prolonging life but prolonging death."[5]

Not only are patients changing their minds in this area, but those in the field of medicine are also doing so. Textbooks now teach doctors that when a patient is confined to bed because of a terminal cancer, it is unwise to push for chemotherapy. Rather, such people should be encouraged to seek treatments that will allay their suffering.[6]

It is interesting that while most people do not want to die in the hospital, many still do. Approximately 50 percent of Americans die in hospitals, and of these, 20 percent die in intensive care units.[7] These numbers need to be compared to a Gallup poll that showed that if people knew they had less than six months to live, more than 90 percent would opt to stay at home rather than pursue aggressive medical treatment.[8] Hospitals, after all, in spite of their best efforts, can be very dehumanizing. They can be dehumanizing when each organ system is taken care of by its own specialist and there is limited emphasis on whole-person treatment. For those who die in the hospital, it is often in the presence of strangers rather than loved ones and friends.

MANY PEOPLE ASK A MORAL QUESTION

I understand that rejecting life-prolonging treatment is equivalent to choosing to die. This raises a moral question: "Doesn't this amount to killing, and if so, isn't that wrong?" I have argued that it is wrong to willfully take human life. We discussed earlier that all human beings are made in God's image, and therefore human life is under God's protection. However, allowing a patient to die is not murder. Granted, it may be wrong to withhold treatment to someone who has a reasonable chance of survival, but when death is inevitable, it is morally right to allow it to come and to refrain from prolonging the dying process. In fact, when God is calling his child home, it may be wrong for us to seek to resist that call. Desiring to prolong life at all costs may in fact be making an idol of life, valuing it more than God himself.

THERE IS BIBLICAL PRECEDENT FOR NOT PROLONGING DEATH

Adding to our assurance that a choice to die is morally acceptable is the example of the apostle who said, "I am ready not only to be imprisoned but even to die in Jerusalem for the name of the Lord Jesus" (Acts 21:13). For Paul, as precious as life was, it was more important to him to give life up if necessary to be faithful to the gospel and to his Lord. Jesus himself illustrated this when he purposely approached his death, knowing it was a crucial part of the Father's plan. Struggling to make a choice in the garden, he prayed, "Father, if you are willing, remove this cup from me. Nevertheless, not my will, but yours, be done" (Luke 22:42). Our Lord placed a higher priority on obeying the Father than resisting death. Then when death came, he submitted to it: "And Jesus cried out again with a loud voice and gave up his spirit" (Matt. 27:50). Actually, a believer is in a win-win situation. The apostle Paul expressed this so succinctly when he wrote: "For to me to live is Christ, and to die is gain" (Phil. 1:21). He valued his earthly life but not to the degree that he valued the Lord and the eternal life he would share in God's presence.

Changing Gears Allows You to Surrender Control

Christians often find it hard to submit fully to God's control over their lives. The longer we live, the more it seems we desire that control. We want to make our own decisions and call the shots. Handing the reins over to someone else counters our innate impulse. But there is a tremendous peace derived from following Proverbs 3:5–6: "Trust in the LORD with all your heart, and do not lean on your own understanding. In all your ways acknowledge him, and he will make straight your paths." In a very real sense changing gears gives us an opportunity to trust the Lord fully. Doing so powerfully affirms faith. In essence we say: "I am giving up control of my life. The time of my death is now totally in God's hands and I rest it there."

Over the years I have heard many patients say just the opposite. When I ask them to consider the benefits and burdens concerning life-sustaining treatment, they tell me to continue with aggressive treatment as long as possible. They believe that by accepting such treatment, they are leaving their lives in God's hands. I have never been able to understand this thinking. It appears to me that this approach is about maintaining control rather than surrendering it. Choosing to stop life-sustaining treatment is often a greater act of surrender than deciding to continue it.

Some say that changing gears is "playing God." I do not believe that is true. Rather it is turning over the reins of our life to God, trusting him fully, and honoring his sovereignty over our lives.[9] It allows God to be God.

Changing Gears Honors the Gospel

Christians believe that by Jesus' death and resurrection, he defeated death. We need not fear death, and we need not fight it to the bitter end. It is consistent with the gospel to say, "I know that I am soon to leave this earth; God is calling me home. Rather than struggling to resist his call, I will rest my soul in the arms of Jesus and trust him fully." We can do this when we change gears.

Believers for the last two thousand years have found this peace at the time of death. Nazi victim Dietrich Bonhoeffer's last words were a testimony of his confidence in God's Word; he told two prison guards who came to take him to be executed, "For you it is an end, for me a beginning." When death approached, Bonhoeffer simply rested in the truth of the gospel. I have rarely seen patients who are fighting death with all possible technology truly rest in God. Changing gears and choosing not to fight death may be a unique opportunity to show those who are looking on just how much peace we have in Jesus. It may be our final opportunity this side of heaven to affirm the truth of the gospel.

❧ ☙

As a Christian physician dedicated to preserve life, I believe strongly that when there is genuine hope to recover an acceptable quality of life, we should fight death as an enemy and pursue health with all the wisdom, strength, and technology that God allows. At the same time, when death is inevitable, let us view death as a defeated enemy and not resist it. Let us change gears, stop fighting, accept it, and thank God for the hope we have in Jesus.

When to Change Gears

Having considered why to change gears, we need to answer the question of when to switch to comfort care. I will share a wide range of factors we need to consider, including physical, emotional, spiritual, and social issues. I will then review some of the reasons popular culture advocates to switch gears, and finally I will present a uniquely Christian approach.

Before we go further, let me assure you that I don't think these decisions are easy. There are no simple answers that are right for everyone. I suggest that you approach these matters with great humility and dependence on the wisdom that God promises. Start with prayer, remembering: "If any of you lacks wisdom, let him ask God, who gives generously to all without reproach, and it will be given him" (James 1:5). Then use the same procedure you have followed in making other major choices in your lifetime. Gather as much information as you can, get the opinions of experts, and call for the spiritual leaders of your church to meet with you to pray both for healing and for wisdom. Be willing to talk openly. If you are a Christian and non-Christians are involved, this is an opportunity to speak of your faith and the peace that you have in Christ Jesus.

Physical Considerations

We must first acquire a correct diagnosis, which might require a lot of testing. At times, a patient of mine has resisted this, telling me: "Doc, don't put me through a lot of tests. I am dying; just let me go."

Jay was one of these. He was in his midseventies, a long-term smoker, and a prime candidate to develop lung cancer. Along with shortness of breath and other symptoms, his X-rays suggested he was in the final stages of lung cancer. When I advised a biopsy to confirm what we suspected, he strongly rejected it, repeatedly telling me not to do anything more but to allow him to die in peace. His wife, however, eventually convinced him to permit the biopsy. To everyone's surprise the test revealed he had a very treatable form of lymph node cancer. A mere twenty-four hours into treatment, he was feeling better, and eventually he was able to live an active life. Jay tragically died five years later in a motorcycle accident, but his earlier testing and correct diagnosis enabled him to spend those five fruitful years with his wife and family.

Having a correct diagnosis will lead to the next crucial step in making the changing gears decision: determining the prognosis. Your doctor will tell you what you can expect your future condition to be like with and without treatment. You will get a description of treatment options, including the burden associated with such treatments. Your doctors will also talk about the chances of any treatment's success, including what that "success" means. For example, you may be told that 70 percent of patients survive certain types of neurosurgery, but you may not be told that two-thirds of survivors end up totally dependent in a nursing home. That additional information may alter your view of "success." It is wise to consider the possible and the more likely side effects of the various treatments available.

Besides getting information from physicians, it's helpful to get their professional recommendations of what you should do. Ask the doctor what she would do if this were her mother or her husband.

One difficulty that I often face when working with a critically ill patient is that each organ involved requires its own specialist. It is not uncommon for a pulmonary physician to be handling the respirator, a cardiologist to be managing the heart, a neurologist to be looking at the brain, etc. I have seen situations where a specialist will tell patients they can survive a problem they are treating. As a result the patient and family take renewed hope and pursue aggressive care when they might have made another decision if they had considered the whole picture. It is helpful to have a primary care physician involved at all times, since it is his job to keep the big picture in view even while specialists are handling many of the details.

Prognosis is inevitably age-dependent. It should be evident that a child who survives a critical illness by aggressive treatment has the potential for many years of productive life. If a ninety-year-old survives a critical illness, it will not be too long before a new problem develops that will eventually prove fatal. Aggressive treatment is often more appropriate for the young.

Bioethicist Daniel Callahan gives very wise guidelines. He says we should change gears to focus on comfort care when:

1. Death is a strong probability.
2. Available treatments for a fatal condition will likely extend pain and suffering.
3. Successful treatment is more likely to bring extended unconsciousness or advanced dementia than cure.
4. Available treatments increase the probability of a death "hooked up to machines," when the patient would have preferred otherwise.[10]

EMOTIONAL CONSIDERATIONS

As you would expect, the emotional responses to life's last days are quite varied. Many people facing the end of life have a serene peace and are resigned that their earthly lives are over. I've seen the opposite response, too; patients become deeply saddened and anxious about being near the end. Some have a fear of dying. This may be true of Christians as well as unbelievers. Others want to live a little longer in order to accomplish one more thing. They may want to experience an important event: a visit from a relative; a granddaughter's wedding; or their one-hundredth birthday. Following the anticipated experience, they come to peace quickly and no longer try to fight death.

Elizabeth Kübler-Ross, a psychiatrist who was one of the first to investigate the emotions of dying, described stages people experience when facing a terminal illness.[11] She mentions denial and isolation, anger, bargaining, depression, and finally acceptance. It is helpful to recognize where one is in these stages of grief. To do so may allow a more rapid transition to acceptance. Once there, it will be easier to comfortably change gears.

Denial. Even though it's clear that life may soon be over, people often deny that their life is coming to an end. Simply being human prompts us to hope for a long and healthy life on earth. When ill, it's natural to believe we can recover, just as we have in the past. There is nothing wrong with having hope. However, hope taken to an extreme or placed exclusively in this life becomes an unhealthy form of denial. Though I have never seen such an extreme reaction to dying as one pastor witnessed, it is easy for me to believe his account.

He told me of a conversation he had had with an eighty-two-year-old woman, who was lying in a hospital bed in a cardiac ward. Her medical record indicated she was rapidly dying of heart failure. Her appearance, however, displayed the extent of her denial. Dressed in a frilly pink bed jacket, her nails freshly polished, her hair carefully set, she spoke in a tiny but seductive voice. She talked of her past independence, the business she formerly owned, and the automobile she drove until she entered the hospital. Recognizing all those as signs of denial, when the pastor prayed, he quoted Paul: "Though our outer self is wasting away, our inner self is being renewed day by day" (2 Cor. 4:16). As he said good-bye and turned to leave, the woman shouted at him, "But my outer nature isn't wasting away!" Within forty-eight hours she passed away, having refused to face her dying.

The problem with denial is that it prevents adequate preparation for what is inevitably to come.

Think about a father dying of widespread cancer. One son comes in and says, "Dad, let's get going. Summer is coming, and I know you will be up and back on the golf course with me. We will have a great time together." Dad knows very well that won't happen, but how is he to respond? The other son comes in and says, "Dad, I really hate to see you like this. I know that the end is going to come, but I want you to know how much I've appreciated all of the rounds of golf we enjoyed over the years and I am sure going to miss you." Can you see how the second son's comment is likely to start a rich conversation as father and son affirm their love for each other?

Dr. Kübler-Ross does not include fear in her list of emotional responses. I have observed, however, that much of denial stems from fear. Hospice nurse Deborah Howard comments: "They fear pain; they fear the progression of their deterioration and disability; and they fear the loss of control over personal decisions. But what they fear most is the act of dying. Most patients tell me that they are not afraid of death itself."[12] But the patient might indeed fear death, or the family might fear a future that does not include their loved one.

Anger. It is only natural to be angry at disease and death, and for that matter, at the Devil and sin, which ultimately stand behind death. It is also possible to be angry with the healthcare team, caregivers, and loved ones who disappoint. When experiencing that anger, it is good to identify it and make sure that you do not dwell in it. Scripture warns us not to sin in our anger (Eph. 4:26). We must be particularly careful when we are angry with God; doubting his goodness is often destructive and at times sinful.

Bargaining. Anytime you do something in order to get a certain result, you may be bargaining. This might be good; it might be bad. If you choose to try a new form of chemotherapy or attempt radical surgery, the treatment might be very successful, and you may be glad with your choice. Some people try experimental medical treatments or something from the world of alternative

medicine. You might seek a consultation from a renowned specialist across the country. Any of these may be appropriate, but you
should be careful not to be persuaded to try something unrea-
sonable, such as an Internet site that promises a cure or a clinic
in the third world that boasts great success. Bargaining may also
involve God. Many people at this time have a deep experience
with God that renews their faith and trust. Others seek to use
God to accomplish what they want. They may make a pledge to
God, promising to do or give something if he will heal them. It
is always wrong to seek to bargain with or manipulate God to do
what we want. When we do so, we are trying to take control of
our lives and to use God to accomplish our purposes. Ultimately
bargaining with God is a failure to trust him.

Depression. Almost everything associated with death can be
depressing. It is natural to feel depressed in our spirits when
we are dealing with the dying. Recall how Jesus wept when
standing at the tomb of Lazarus. He knew Lazarus would be
raised from the dead, but when he confronted all of the losses
associated with death and how contrary death is to the original
intent of creation, Jesus wept. It is good to be sad and to feel
the intensity of our losses. Ecclesiastes reminds us that there is
"a time to mourn . . ." (Eccles. 3:4). On the other hand, if that
mourning goes too far and paralyzes one's will and ability to relate
to others, it will become counterproductive. At that point the
depression needs to be confronted, and it possibly will require
professional help.

Acceptance. The struggle to stay alive can be wearisome. You
are worn out by repeated trips to the doctor or the hospital as
well as weary of taking pills and suffering their side effects. Not
feeling well wears on you so that you eventually long to escape
the confines of your sick or aging body. The list of things you still
want to accomplish has gotten shorter. Weary of living, heaven
looks pretty good. You have come to accept death with great
equanimity.

Some may progress through these emotions one at a time.
Others may experience them all at the same time or seem to

bounce from one to another randomly. I have observed situations where each person involved was at a different stage of these emotional responses. Sally was dying of lung cancer and had peace with her decision to sign up for hospice and not try to fight it further. Her husband could not forgive himself for years of smoking in her presence (anger). Her son was making plans for the entire family to take a cruise together to Hawaii (denial). Her daughter had decided to go back to her church so that God would hear her prayers for her mother (bargaining). Sally's best friend refused to visit and was spending too much time at home by herself (depression).

Spiritual Considerations

As a Christian as well as a physician, I am very aware of how a person's spiritual outlook influences the decision to change gears. Some without eternal hope cannot give up. It would mean the end of everything they know, or worse yet it would mean eternal judgment.

Ken was dying slowly of emphysema. He had been on a breathing machine for over six months at home under the care of his wife and family. Every month or so some physical problem would require his being hospitalized. He was tired of living that way, but he told me he was not ready to die. We talked about changing gears, which in his case meant my providing comfort treatment at his home but no more admissions to the hospital. He was intrigued by the idea of gently letting go, and he wanted to die at home—but he couldn't give up. One day he confided in me that he had recommitted his life to Christ and that he was now ready to let go any further efforts to keep him alive. The next time he was discharged from the hospital, he indicated he would ask not to be brought back. Because he was spiritually at peace with God, he was at peace with dying.

For some people who have not had a personal relationship with God through Jesus Christ, being aware of a terminal illness gives them an opportunity to make a decision to trust their eternal well-being to God. I have seen many believers with a passion for God graciously let go of the things of the world and gently slip into the Lord's presence. It is this spiritual preparation that takes the sting out of death.

Social Considerations

How we die has a wide impact on others. John Donne alluded to this:

> No man is an island, entire of itself; every man is a piece of the continent, a part of the main. If a clod be washed away by the sea, Europe is the less, as well as if a promontory were, as well as if a manor of thy friend's or of thine own were: any man's death diminishes me, because I am involved in mankind, and therefore never send to know for whom the bell tolls; it tolls for thee.[13]

Joni Eareckson Tada encountered a young lady who was terminally ill and wrestling with the question of whether to accept a breathing machine. Tada urged her to be aware that her decision was not her own—that it would influence many other people.[14] Though the choice to change gears belongs to the dying and cannot be dictated by everyone's whim, there are times when the feelings of others should be taken into account. Al, a middle-aged man, was dying of cancer. Both Al and his wife knew he was beyond hope of recovery, and they accepted it. Because their twenty-year-old daughter was struggling with his dying, Al requested that we do everything we could to prolong his life. This was the appropriate choice. He did this as a final gift to his daughter.

I do not deal with dying children, but I recognize how agonizing it is for parents to give up their little ones. I am sympathetic to parents who choose aggressive care to the end for their children. Still, though, I would hate to feel that a loved one's failure to let go would prolong the suffering of the dying.

Biblical Considerations

For years I have struggled with the question of when Christians should choose to forgo aggressive treatment and graciously accept death as God's call. In other words, when do we treat death as an enemy and when do we accept it as a defeated enemy? Clearly, we need to think through the physical, emotional, spiritual, and social contexts. After considering these, however, Christians will still need to consider what God's Word says. I have seen believers decide to change gears for a number of reasons that I find difficult to reconcile with Scripture. Here are some of the reasons I have heard and what I feel is a biblical response:

Fig. 8.1 Unbiblical Reasons to Switch to Comfort Care

Concern	Biblical Answer
I will lose control.	God wants us to give him control.
I fear pain and suffering.	Our trials can be productive.
I will lose my dignity.	Our dignity is rooted in being made in God's image.
I fear death.	The gospel frees us from this fear.

Note that all of these concerns are more centered on us and not on God and his glory.

What, then, should a Christian consider when determining the time to switch to comfort care rather than cure? I do not believe that the Bible gives us any clear guidance. In my study of the Scriptures, though, I find an emphasis on serving others. For example, the apostle Paul has a passion to glorify God by encouraging others in their faith till the moment of his death:

> For to me to live is Christ, and to die is gain. If I am to live in the flesh, that means fruitful labor for me. Yet which I shall choose I cannot tell. I am hard pressed between the two. My desire is to depart and be with Christ, for that is far better. But to remain in the flesh is more necessary on your account. Convinced of this, I know that I will remain and continue with you all, for your progress and joy in the faith, so that in me you may have ample cause to glory in Christ Jesus, because of my coming to you again. (Phil. 1:21–26)

Personally, when I see my ability to encourage and serve others greatly diminish, I will see that as a signal to change gears. I am fully aware, however, that not all people are able to serve others. They are totally dependent, and I do not want to discount the value of their lives. These dear souls enrich the lives of those around them. They are made in God's image, and have all of the dignity implied by that. It is a privilege to serve them.

I also recognize that, as I discussed in strategy 1, the nature of our service will change over the years. I may not be practicing medicine, teaching classes, or writing articles. I may be dependent on some life-sustaining technology and on my caregivers. The nature of my service may be to encourage others and pray for them. If I can serve others in this way, I will not be ready to change gears, and I will pursue life-prolonging treatment.

If, however, my life is not of use to others, and there is little likelihood of that situation improving, I do not want my own life to be prolonged. While I would not want anyone to take my life, I would not want life-sustaining treatment either.

WHAT ABOUT NON-CHRISTIANS?

When I speak on these issues, one very common question is whether we should handle nonbelievers differently from believers. I appreciate the wisdom of C. S. Lewis:

> [Some say] that death ought not to be final, that there ought to be a second chance. I believe that if a million chances were likely to do good, they would be given. But a master often knows, when boys and parents do not, that it is really useless to send a boy in for a certain examination again. Finality must come sometime, and it does not require a very robust faith to believe that omniscience knows when.[15]

Bill was dying of a rapidly growing cancer of his tongue. He could not swallow and was having trouble breathing. At the end, Bill was miserable and wanted to die. He had abused his body for years. His godly sister had prayed for him for years and tried to share with him the good news of Jesus. She had been continually rebuffed. With tears in her eyes, she begged me to do anything possible to prolong his life so that she could have one more chance to plead with him to trust Jesus. With tears in my eyes, I had to tell her that there was nothing more I could do; he was in God's hands. We needed to trust God to do what was right.

How to Change Gears

Having considered all of these factors and made the decision to change gears, the next question arises: "How do I go about doing it?" There are a number of steps you can take.

Talk to Your Family

If you do not include your family when making your decision to turn to comfort care, it is crucial that you talk about it afterward. You can have rich days as you review your life and your relationships with them. Make sure you let them know the reasons behind your decision. Be aware that your candor in talking about death may surprise people, but your courage to speak of your own death will help put them at ease. They will likely find it a relief to be able to talk openly with you. It will likely give you an opportunity to share your faith and the reason for your hope of eternal life with those who do not know Christ.

Talk to Your Physician

I always appreciate patients who schedule an appointment to discuss end-of-life care. This is a critical step and should never be tacked on to the end of another appointment. It is essential to talk with your doctor not only about when you would want to change gears but how you can do it.

Prepare Advanced Directives

Advance directives are legal documents that indicate the kind of medical care you would want if you were to become unable to express your wishes. Everyone should have advance directives prepared early in their lives. At the latest, you should do so when you make a decision to change gears. Since the laws regulating advance directives vary from state to state, I can only give some general suggestions. You can find out what your state requires and obtain appropriate forms through a local hospital. Otherwise you can find this information on the Internet site Putitinwriting. org. Advance directives generally fall into two categories: living wills and limited powers of attorney for medical purposes. Living wills are narrow in their application, and I do not find them of much value by themselves, but coupled with a power of attorney, they are more helpful.

Through a limited power of attorney, you can accomplish several important things. First, you can appoint someone who can make medical decisions for you if you become incapacitated. Second, these documents often allow you to stipulate who decides if you are incapacitated. Finally, they give you the opportunity to give some direction to the individual you appoint as your power of attorney. As you prepare this document, I suggest the following:

1. Appoint an individual to serve as your power of attorney who will make decisions in line with your own values and instructions. In many cases your spouse knows you best and will make the same choices you would make. But sometimes a spouse may be less inclined to "let go" than you would be. You may want someone else who can be more objective. If you do not choose your spouse, you should explain to her that you do not want her to feel the burden of making such hard decisions. In addition, you should discuss your spouse's sensitivities with your chosen power of attorney and emphasize that if your spouse needs more time for closure, you are willing to have some life-prolonging treatment to allow for that.

2. Direct that your power of attorney and your primary care physician must jointly make the decision as to whether you are incapacitated. Indicate that if the two of them do not agree, they should appoint a third party, who is mutually acceptable, to make the decision. You may instruct

that the individual be a professional such as a psychiatrist, neurologist, or pastor.

3. Do not give specific directions for your medical care. Many state forms give a check-off list that includes such things as resuscitation, ventilator, and artificial nutrition and hydration. I do not suggest you indicate a preference for or against these. It seems much wiser to leave those boxes blank and give your power of attorney full freedom to make the wisest choices he or she can. Then write a paragraph indicating your values. This allows your power of attorney to be much more focused on the context of your condition rather than on procedures.

If you give instructions that are very specific, they may have results that you never intended. For example, I have seen patients brought to the emergency room over the years in comas with life-threatening pneumonias. They are put on a ventilator and started on antibiotics. Within several days they regain consciousness and leave the hospital doing well. If they had checked a box on their advance directive box that indicated "no ventilator," they would likely not have survived. When I review advance directive forms and see this box checked, I always ask the patients if they would want to be put on to a ventilator in the above situation. No one has ever said that they envisioned a scenario like the above when they filled out the forms. Rather, they respond: "I only meant that I did not want to be kept on the machine forever." I gently tell them that is not what checking the "no ventilator" box indicates.

My own power of attorney names my wife, Dorothy, as my decision maker, and I indicate that I want her to have full discretion over all decisions. I have not checked off any specific medical procedures; rather, I include the following statement:

> I am happy for technology to be used so long as there is reasonable hope of it allowing me to serve others. But if

for physical, mental, emotional, or spiritual reasons it is unlikely I will be able to serve others, I do not want that technology.

This approach is consistent with the gospel and would be something like what the biblical writers would write were they faced with the technological options we now have.

Consider Hospice or Palliative Care

Most communities provide palliative care and hospice. These are organizations designed to provide comfort care when cure may not be possible. They are an excellent way to help people implement a decision to change gears. Hospices repeatedly emphasize that their care is not fundamentally about dying—it is about living the best possible life right up till the end. Some hospices have residences where patients can live. Most provide services to people in their own home, a hospital, or a nursing home. It is my experience that some of the finest nurses are attracted to these associations. Hospice and palliative care groups are required to attend to the needs of the whole person, not just the medical needs. They usually have social workers, chaplains, health aides, and lay volunteers to assist the dying and their caregivers in just about every way imaginable. Some hospices are explicitly Christian. Some are willing to support whatever faith a patient has. There are a few, however, that are committed to a non- or even anti-Christian understanding of spirituality, and of these the Christian must be wary.

Both hospice and palliative care offer extensive expertise in comfort care. The major difference is that hospice is for those who have decided to forgo all treatment designed for cure. Palliative care allows you to pursue curative treatment even while you desire to minimize pain and other symptoms. It encourages you to prepare for death if the treatment does not cure the disease. Palliative care allows you to "hope for the best while you prepare for the worst."

Sign Do Not Resuscitate (DNR) Orders

All hospitals and residential health facilities are required to inquire on admission if a patient desires resuscitation in the event that his heart or breathing stops. Signing a DNR is another practical way to implement a decision to change gears.

Do Not Call 911

We have an amazing emergency response system in this country. Its modern equipment and well-trained personnel are excellent at maintaining and preserving life. However, unless you can show them a signed DNR order when they arrive, their job is to use all means possible to support and prolong life. I am thankful for the invaluable service they render to our communities but wish that those who are terminally ill had access to other emergency medical care to provide comfort, though not life-sustaining, treatment.

Review Medical Care

After a patient has decided to change gears, I carefully review all of their medical care. This is one step that is easy to overlook. I am amazed at how often patients who have decided to die comfortably at home and not be aggressively treated are still taking medications intended to prolong life. I know that the distinction between these two is often blurred, but still it is wise to discontinue any life-sustaining treatment. There are a few drugs that promote comfort without at the same time prolonging life. These should be continued. On the other hand, there are many drugs, like most chemotherapies, that may prolong life at the price of comfort.

Fran, a ninety-three-year-old retired nurse, was in the final stages of life. She was convinced the end was soon to come and insisted that nothing be done to prolong her life. She called me to her home one night and announced she had gone to bed for the last time. She had arranged to have nurse friends with her around the clock. I assured her we would not do anything but support her and maintain her comfort. If she were to become anxious, short of breath, or in pain, we would give morphine under her tongue. We reviewed each of her medications and categorized them as life prolonging or comfort giving. We stopped the drugs that would only prolong her life but kept up those which would contribute to comfort. She was pleased. We prayed together and committed her to the Lord. She went into a coma three days later and died two days after that. I feel that she died well.

Conclusion

For the Christian, death has been defeated. If we accept that and choose to forgo what is so often death-delaying medical treatment, we can have some time to bring closure to our lives and prepare more to enter the presence of God. I have found that God can be glorified and some of the tragedy of death can be minimized when we change gears and resign ourselves to inevitable death, rather than fighting it to the bitter end.

Prayer

Gracious Father, how very difficult these choices are. Lord, I want to honor you by doing what is right. By your Spirit lead me to make the right choices as I approach the end of my life for the glory of your holy name. Amen

===== MEDITATION =====

All the way my Savior leads me;
What have I to ask beside?
Can I doubt his tender mercy,
Who through life has been my guide?
Heav'nly peace, divinest comfort,
Here by faith in him to dwell;
For I know, whate'er befall me,
Jesus doeth all things well.

All the way my Savior leads me,
Cheers each winding path I tread,

Gives me grace for ev'ry trial,
Feeds me with the living bread.
Though my weary steps may falter,
And my soul athirst may be,
Gushing from the rock before me,
Lo, a spring of joy I see!

All the way my Savior leads me—
O the fullness of his love!
Perfect rest to me is promised
In my Father's house above:
When my spirit, clothed, immortal,
Wings its flight to realms of day,
This my song through endless ages:
Jesus led me all the way!

"ALL THE WAY, MY SAVIOR
LEADS ME," FANNY CROSBY
(1875)

Rest in Jesus

What should we expect as death approaches?

What kind of care is appropriate as life ends?

What do we do when someone has second thoughts?

How do we handle death when it is messy?

What can loved ones do for the dying?

Can we simply rest in Jesus?

We now turn our thoughts to death itself. Earlier I described strategies that apply to the last decades of our lives. In the last few chapters I discussed the final months and even weeks. Now we consider the last days and hours before death.

Sid was in his mid-eighties. He had been a believer since he had first heard the gospel in his twenties. He had been married to a fine Christian woman and together they had raised three children, all of whom became Christians. Sid was suffering from pulmonary fibrosis, a slowly progressive scarring of the lungs that is frequently fatal. He had been in the hospital four times in the previous fifteen months with pneumonia and twice had pulled through only with the help of a ventilator. He was getting weaker and weaker. When he went home for the last time, he simply said, "No more." This was his very direct way of indicating that he wanted to change gears. No more aggressive treatment. He was ready to go to be with his Lord. Without his wife, who had died three years earlier, and aware of the seriousness of his deteriorating condition, he had no reason to continue the fight. He also felt he was becoming too much of a burden on his daughter, who lived next door to him. He made his wishes clear to her, and she shared them with the other two children, who lived out of state. Sometime after that, Sid's son came to town to stay with his dad while his sister went away with her husband.

Sid's daughter had only been gone a few days when the son phoned me while I was at the hospital one morning. He told me that he was going to call 911 because Sid's condition was worsening. I explained to him that his father had not wanted that to be done, and suggested he wait the fifteen minutes it would take me to complete rounds and come by the house. Meanwhile he was to try to get in touch with his sister to see what she felt about Sid's being hospitalized. When I arrived at the home, the son met me in the driveway, handed me his cell phone, and said, "Here is my sister—it's between the two of you." She reaffirmed her dad's wishes, explaining that she would be home in about eight hours. When I went in to see Sid, I found him breathing hard, though he was not in great distress (partly because he was on oxygen). He clearly was suffering from pneumonia and a high fever. I explained how to treat the fever and prescribed a concentrated form of morphine. Putting a few drops in Sid's mouth from time to time would prevent what might be the agonizing shortness of breath that he would no doubt experience. The son then called a nurse who was a friend of the family and together they started a bedside vigil. That afternoon the daughter arrived, and Sid was able to acknowledge her presence. He then started to move his hands like he was playing a violin. The family got the message and called a good friend who was a professional violinist. She came over and for eight hours played his favorite hymns over and over again. Sid was at peace, and for most of the time he lay there with a smile on his face. He knew that the Lord was calling, and he was content to answer that call. He died comfortably as the music played. Sid illustrates our ninth and final strategy to finish life well: strategy 9: Rest in Jesus.

We do not naturally associate death with God's glory. Yet that is a theme we see repeatedly in the New Testament. Jesus, Paul, and Peter were all able to die in such a way that God was glorified and honored (John 17:1; 21:19; Phil. 1:20–21). Should that not be one of our strongest aspirations? There is no better way to glorify God in our deaths than by quietly surrendering all control of our lives to him, allowing him to take us home. Having grieved the loss of the pleasant aspects of earthly life, Christians must die focused on the fact that death is not an end but the beginning of a whole new life. It should be a time of both completion and anticipation. It is finally experiencing what true life is all about. Dying for the Christian is always seen in the context of resurrection. It is always filled with hope.

That is not to say that the act of dying is always pretty and nice. We may aspire to a death like Sid's, but that is not always possible. Death can at times be messy and ugly. Though we often speak of dying with dignity, philosopher Oliver O'Donovan reminds us that there is nothing at all dignified about it.[1] We can, however, bring dignity to death. In this chapter I want you to see how the last moments of life can be glorifying to God and what steps you can take to better ensure they are. I first discuss some of the physical aspects involved in dying, then some of the emotional and family issues, and finally some spiritual matters.

Signs of Approaching Death

No death is the same, but there are some features that are common to many. It can be helpful to recognize some of these as the dying process progresses; knowing that these experiences are natural and to be expected can relieve some anxiety.

One of the earliest signs of impending death is a marked increase in fatigue and in longer time spent in sleep. At the same time sleep may be more restless. Painkillers and sedatives can aggravate this restlessness. The fatigue may result in an inability to sustain normal social interactions. The dying may not appreciate a lot of people around and may ask some to leave. They may feel they have already said their good-byes. This goes along with the old Irish tradition of turning to face the wall when death is near. Social withdrawal like this should never give offense, though loved ones may feel a sense of rejection. The time for deep meaningful conversations may be past. As a result of the fatigue, but also contributing to it, is a loss of appetite and thirst. The intestinal tract is shutting down and is not able to accept things by mouth. This is natural, and often promotes comfort rather than feeling bloated by the body's retention of fluids. The terminally ill should be offered food and fluids, but not be forced to take more than they want.

As death becomes closer, circulation slows down. The arms and legs tend to become mottled and cold. Death usually follows within hours, though I have seen this stage last for much longer. Toward the end, breathing will tend to be very irregular; there will be periods of rapid respiration followed by long pauses. Each pause may suggest that death has come, only to have another breath declare life is not over. All through these final hours the patient may become less and less responsive, but it is not uncommon just before death to have a few lucid moments. This is when the patient may say the traditional "last words" or relate a vision of what we as Christians will interpret as heaven. Then the patient dies. Breathing stops, the heart is no longer beating, and an unmistakable pallor comes over the face as the lifeblood is drained out. It is rarely painful, and there is frequently no struggle.[2]

The use of life support and resuscitation can change this usual manner of dying. When a patient is on a ventilator, the usual terminology of death, "cardiopulmonary death," no longer applies. The lungs will continue to receive air indefinitely, and the heart may keep on pumping blood. This has prompted the medical community to create a new definition of death. The concept of "brain death" was initiated in the 1960s. This occurs when the brain has been sufficiently damaged as to be permanently incapable of supporting heart and lung function without machines. While I recognize that there is room for debate, it seems reasonable to say that if the heartbeat is totally dependent on technology and there is no hope for recovery, then the patient is in fact dead. Life is over.

Care When Death Is Immanent

When death is soon to come, one question frequently asked is, "Where does the patient want to die?" Most people want to be in their own homes with their families around them, as was the case with Elmer.

At age ninety-six, Elmer had been living with his daughter, Rose, since his wife died some years before. Now that Rose was retiring and moving out of the area, she hoped he would join her in her new home. This seemed unlikely, however, since his health was failing; it was clear that he would not live much longer. Elmer was moved to a nursing home, but after only one week there, he was admitted to the hospital. At that point he told his daughter that he wanted to get back to the home that they had shared together and die there. Rose did not feel she could change her plans, so she arranged for him to return to the nursing home. He reluctantly agreed. The day he was to be discharged it became clear that he was terminal, so he was kept another day in the hospital. After Elmer survived through that day and was about to be discharged, his daughter had second thoughts. When she told him that she would take him to her home and delay her move, you could see that he was thrilled. Arrangements were made through hospice for a hospital bed and oxygen at home. After being home comfortably with Rose for three days, he died in the presence of his family. Elmer was able to communicate his desires to Rose, and she was willing to respond. I have seen others who desperately wanted to be home with their families but did not want to be a burden, so they chose not to express their desires and instead went to a nursing facility for their final days.

The decision is not always as simple as it was for Elmer. At times the feelings of others must be considered, particularly if young children are involved. A parent who wants to die at home must consider whether this would cause future psychological problems for the children. One other complicating factor is the challenge we have in predicting how long life will last. I have occasionally seen a loving family bring a parent to their house to provide for her during the final days, thinking that death would come within a month or so. Family members sometimes take a leave from work to provide the care the parent needs; they can go without a paycheck for a month, but they do not anticipate the six months it would be before their loved one was called home. It is not uncommon that a relentless downhill course is dramatically slowed once the patient is comfortable being cared for in her own home.

When death is immediately coming, it is essential that the direction of medical care change. This is particularly true when the death occurs in a hospital or nursing home. At no time should the patient be ignored. On the other hand, routine monitoring of vital signs and blood tests is rarely necessary. Certainly, staff should do regular checks and spend as much time as possible with the patient. Stroking the cheek or a hug around the shoulder to provide human contact is more appropriate than checking the temperature and blood pressure.

Second Thoughts

The fear of dying will often lead to second thoughts as the end gets very close. I have repeatedly seen people emphatically state that they do not want aggressive life-prolonging care, and then at the very end ask for it by dialing 911. The causes for these second thoughts are complex. Part of being human is having an intrinsic love of life. At times it is the patient who changes his mind. At other times it is the persuasion by a spouse or child who feels that to do nothing is to give up. At other times it is a well-meaning physician or nurse who offers "one more thing to try." Sometimes a patient is influenced by the manner in which the doctor asks about having further treatment. I have heard doctors of patients who were terminal ask, "Do you want us to try . . . or do you want to die?" People will almost always say that they do not want to die. Perhaps it would be better to remind them, "Now we are at the place we talked about several months ago. Your life is coming to an end; this is where we decided we would continue to provide for your comfort but not do things just to prolong your life."

Annabelle arrived in the emergency room with excruciating chest pain that went through to her back. Her aorta had ruptured! She was flown to a university hospital where her life was saved by heroic emergency surgery. Because the surgeons were unable to repair the entire aneurysm at the time, plans were made to fix the rest later. However, while recovering from the first surgery, she had a cardiac arrest. She was resuscitated and required a ventilator for six weeks. Annabelle finally did well, and after a month in a nursing home, doctors were able to do the second surgery. Again she was dependent on a ventilator for several weeks after the operation. After three months of convalescence in the nursing home she recovered enough to get home. The first time I saw her after the surgery, she greeted me by saying, "I will never go on that horrible machine another time."

Three years later Annabelle developed severe pneumonia and was rushed to another hospital where she was placed on a ventilator in the emergency room. After she was transferred to the hospital where I attend, she continued to be on "that horrible machine" for another month. Once free of the ventilator, she repeated, "Never again." She was transferred out of intensive care where she continued to recover over the next two weeks. She was careful to sign documents stating that she did not want to be resuscitated or to be placed on any machines. One day I saw that her condition had deteriorated and she was struggling to breathe. I said to her, "Annabelle, this is the day we talked about that would eventually come. We could keep you going for a bit longer on the breathing machine, but we already decided not to do that. Instead we will do what you requested and keep you comfortable." Her response was, "No, put me back on the machine." Before I did anything, I called her husband, who begged me to wait till he arrived at the hospital to talk with her. By the time he arrived, she had lapsed into a coma. Since she was no longer competent to make a decision, he simply said, "No ventilator." Annabelle died comfortably within the hour. Before she died however, she squeezed his hand, which was enough to assure him that he had made the right decision. One has to have a deep respect for a desire to live; but at times it goes too far.

There are times, however, when even comfort care demands a very aggressive response. Mac was in his nineties. He was dying of progressive kidney failure and was cared for by hospice at home. I knew that his family was struggling with letting him go, but Mac had made it clear that he did not want any aggressive care or life prolongation. One night when I was not on call, he became very short of breath. When my partner was called, he told the family to call 911. When I arrived at the hospital the next morning to reassume Mac's care, I was very upset when I saw that he had been admitted to intensive care. I got there minutes after Mac breathed his last. He had been extremely short of breath at home, and the family could not stand to see him die that way. He had been placed on a machine that helped his breathing, called a BiPAP. While not as uncomfortable as a ventilator, it was enough to ensure his comfort but not prolong his life. I was glad that my partner had been on call, for I may not have suggested Mac be admitted to the hospital. In retrospect I feel Mac was handled appropriately. This was not a case of following unwise "second thoughts," but rather thoughtfully providing compassionate care.

When Death Isn't Pretty

Many stories in this book give the impression that death is always a beautiful, serene experience. Unfortunately, that is not the case. Death often can be nasty and messy. We must remember that death is still the result of sin, and it still belongs to the domain of

Satan. Though Christ has defeated it, death is outside the circle of God's holiness. God never promised us an easy death. John Donne said shortly before his death: "God doth not say, Live well, and thou shalt die well, that is an easy and quiet death; but [God says] Live well here, and thou shalt live well for ever."[3] There are many challenges to dying well; I would like to discuss how to face some of them.

Spiritual Doubt

The many losses associated with the end of life can lead us to doubt some of the truths we know about God. This doubt may accompany depression and be characterized by a lack of hope, purpose, and joy. Some people may be irritable with others and feel disconnected from loved ones and even from God himself. Prayer may seem futile. Times of refreshment previously spent quietly in God's presence may seem dry.[4] This can cast a cloud of spiritual doubt over the end of life.

Along with doubt will often come fear, even for committed Christians. It is helpful to acknowledge that a fear of death is not always a sign of spiritual weakness. Christians can have a legitimate fear of dying even when they have no fear of death. We must be careful to respond compassionately to those who experience that fear. We must not assume that they should be so focused on heaven that they are not grieved by what they are leaving on earth.

When my good friend Emma had colon cancer, she tended to dwell anxiously on the prospect of dying even though the cancer had apparently been cured. Her hope for a future eternal life didn't prevent her from being reluctant to leave this one. She felt that this ambivalence was a sign of spiritual weakness. Putting my hand on her shoulder I said, "Oh, Emma, of course it is not. God has blessed you with a godly husband; you have two lovely children and five delightful grandchildren. He has given you a love of life that many have never experienced. To expect you to want to leave these gifts does an injustice to God's goodness to you." A desire to continue to live does not mean you are spiritually weak.

This fear of dying provides us one more opportunity to trust God to provide what we need. Billy Graham wrote, "He has taken away the fear of death for those who trust in Him. We do not need to be ashamed of our fear, but we can rest assured that He will give us strength when we have none of our own, courage when we are cowardly, and comfort when we are hurting."[5]

Even our Lord himself did not look forward to death. Recall in the garden when he prayed, "My Father, if it be possible, let this cup pass from me; nevertheless, not as I will, but as you will" (Matt. 26:39). Jesus did not embrace death any more than we would. Nevertheless he placed a higher priority on obeying his Father than on his emotional response to death. In meditating on this passage, Sir Thomas Moore wrote, "Fear is not reprehensible as long as reason does not struggle against fear."[6]

I have also seen cases where a fear of death represents uncertainty about the goodness of God. If that is the situation, it may be helpful to reflect back on the many times we have experienced God working in our lives. Should remembering these not strengthen us for the challenge of dying? Puritan Richard Baxter wrote, "Never did God break his promise with me. Never did he fail me, or forsake me. And shall I now distrust him at last?"[7] Dr. V. Raymond Edman of Wheaton College was famous for his counsel: "Do not doubt in the dark what God has shown you in the light." The apostle John reminds us that "There is no fear in love, but perfect love casts out fear . . ." (1 John 4:18). Recall strategy 3: Treasure God's Love. It may be helpful to talk to others of God's great love and to remind ourselves how clearly that love is seen in the cross and in the message of the gospel.

If we are in a season of doubt, it is helpful to repeatedly quote some of the promises of the Bible. John 3:16, John 5:24, Romans 8:32, Romans 8:37–39, and 1 John 3:1–2 are good places to start. The saints of a bygone era faced with spiritual doubt would repeatedly pray, "Lord be merciful to me, a sinner." Casting our souls on the Lord for his mercy can reassure our faith. It reminds us that what counts is not what we have done; it's simply trusting what he has done.

Emotional Ambivalence

In my years of attending to dying people, I have learned that the key word to understanding the emotional response to death is *ambivalence*. It describes Larry's reaction. I was with him two days before he died. Having developed cancer several years earlier, he chose to ignore it, even though he knew that it would eventually kill him. He did not want anything to do with surgery or with doctors, myself included. One day his wife called and said he was in great pain, and he wondered if I would come by and see him. I saw him at home that night and found him very weak, having been writhing in pain all that day. It was clear he was dying, and I told him so. "But I don't want to die!" he said. I told him I could identify with that since I didn't either. I explained that we did not have any way to prolong his life but could certainly do a lot to keep him comfortable. We discussed the reality that the only option to not dying was to continue to suffer as he was, and with that in view, perhaps death was not such a bad alternative. Larry grunted and said, "I guess so." Such is the ambivalence of being close to death. We get to the point where we hate the disease and all that is involved in our treatment, yet we still want to live.

Social Conflict

It saddens me that as difficult as the end of life is, it can be made even tougher when there is unresolved family conflict. Mildred was over one hundred when she lay dying. It was not her age, but a tragic accident that would eventually take her. Her two sons added greatly to the pain and emotional turmoil of her final days. Never having resolved a conflict, they had not spoken to each other for years. Despite their mother's condition and her pleas, they refused to reconcile. At the end she never saw her younger son, who refused to be where his brother was, and the older brother refused to leave his mother's side. While some conflicts have a long history, others arise only at the time of death. The children may disagree on end-of-life decisions. One may want resuscitation, while another does not. It is difficult for everyone involved when some members of the family will not let go and at times will even make the patient feel guilty about dying.

Physical Suffering

There are many ways that physical pain and suffering can make dying difficult. At times the difficulty comes from the intensity of the pain, but at others it is simply due to how long it takes to die. Everyone involved might be prepared for immediate death, but they are not prepared for a patient to live on and on. Ben was dying of emphysema. He had made all of the difficult decisions and had made it clear that he did not want resuscitation, a ventilator, or any aggressive care. One day he was admitted to the hospital with a severe pneumonia and was in a coma. His children knew that he would not live long. Initially, they were with him twenty-four hours a day, even though he was not responding to them. Since he was receiving neither medications nor feedings, I expected him to die at any moment. But he didn't. Ben lived on for almost two weeks. Eventually his children spent very little time with him, and he ended up dying alone.

In some cases it is not the duration but the intensity of the physical distress that makes a person's last days so hard. Inadequate treatment of distressing symptoms such as pain, shortness of breath, vomiting, diarrhea, insomnia, or anxiety may contribute to a difficult death. Means are available to alleviate or at least reduce the intensity of these conditions, but tragically they are not always attended to, and in spite of our best efforts at palliative care some patients will suffer toward the end. At times this occurs because of poor medical practice and inattention or even insensitivity of caregivers. Hospital nurses may not respond to call lights. Hospice nurses may have too many patients to care for at one time. Physicians may not have proper training in the use of symptom-limiting drugs. In other situations the patient or her caregivers may not communicate the degree of distress to the responsible parties who, had they known, might have done something to relieve it.

Sometimes loved ones will have to speak up and make it clear that the patient is in distress and needs help. They should not always assume that the right people are aware of the patient's suffering. Unfortunately, it is still true that the "squeaky wheel gets the oil." I work with dedicated nurses, but I still get calls from family members to tell me their loved one is suffering and the nurses are not responding. If you ever have questions about symptoms that are not adequately controlled, I recommend requesting a consult from a physician who specializes in palliative care if one is available in your area. If not, it's wise to request second opinions on what is the best way to manage a suffering patient.

But this still leaves the question of what do when someone is getting the best possible medical care but is still suffering. Thankfully, these cases are rarely seen. There are several alternatives. One of them is called "terminal sedation." This amounts to sedating a patient so that she is not sufficiently awake to feel pain. It is similar to being given a general anesthetic during surgery. The patient is kept asleep until death occurs. This practice is somewhat controversial since patients will not be able to take oral feedings or fluids to keep them alive. In my mind, "terminal sedation" is an ethical option. Another option is "voluntarily stopping eating and drinking." I believe it is acceptable to suggest to a dying patient that if she chooses not to eat or drink, it may allow for a quicker death. It would be wrong to refuse to feed someone but not wrong for a dying person to choose not to eat. This is not suicide, but rather a choice not to prolong the death. Recall that a loss of appetite is natural as death approaches, and that forcing oneself to eat or being forced to eat by another often adds to the discomfort.

Much more problematic than "terminal sedation" are two other options for alleviating chronic end-of-life suffering: euthanasia and physician-assisted suicide. Currently, physician-assisted suicide is a legal option in the United States only in Oregon, Washington, and Montana, but most states have legal initiatives that might broaden this option. Though I am sympathetic to the plight of those who are dying in a difficult way, I do not believe that physician-assisted suicide is an acceptable option for them. There is a vast difference between allowing someone to die without providing life-prolonging treatment and actually killing them. Scripture makes it clear that only God can determine the time of death and it is sinful for us to take such a decision into our own hands. In reality, the most common reason those in Oregon who have elected physician-assisted suicide give is not the suffering or even fear of it but the disdain for the loss of control.[8] The Christian attitude is far different from this. For a believer, death should be an occasion of surrendering, not of maintaining control. No matter how difficult death may be, it is not right to take our lives into our own hands and proactively end them.

What Can Loved Ones Do?

"Let me know how I can help" is a statement folks often say as death approaches. Though I know people are well-meaning, I don't think it is a good thing to say. We are essentially adding to the burden of people who are already overwhelmed. Think for a moment of what our request entails: we are asking them to evaluate our abilities and interests, think through a list of things that need to be done, and then take the initiative to contact us to tell us what to do and how to do it.[9] At times it is simply best to identify something that you can do and do it.

Spend Time with the Dying

Most people appreciate a human presence when they are dying. It is important though that visitors take their cues from the dying as to what they should do. Some people will want to talk, reminiscing about the past or engaging in serious discussion. At such times, it is perfectly fine to share past humorous experiences and be free to laugh together. Other people will want to have someone present, but remain silent. If you find that you are in that situation, you might want to have something to read to occupy your time and thoughts. Some, like my friend Sid, appreciate quiet music. Others have asked visitors to sing hymns with them or read the lyrics of familiar songs. I know that, for me, I would not appreciate someone sitting in my room watching TV. If the patient is not in the mood for conversation, he may appreciate someone reading to him. Many excellent books are appropriate for such times—but nothing can take the place of the Bible. If your church supports such a practice, you might observe the Lord's Supper. This is a wonderful way to reassure people of Christ's love and to remind them that he died to take the sting out of their death. And, of course, there will always be opportunities to pray together. Tenderly touching someone is often of great value; people may welcome hugs when you come and go, but they may also appreciate your just sitting there holding their hand, rubbing their neck, or stroking their forehead or feet.

If you get into deeper discussion on the meaning of death or even the meaning of suffering, do not be too quick to give superficial answers. It is often more appropriate to sit and wonder at the wisdom of God and to encourage trust in him. One phrase that is frequently used in this situation is, "I know how you feel." In his insightful book about his own struggles, John Feinberg points out how insensitive that statement can be.[10] The fact is that we do not really know how anyone else feels. Even if we have been through similar situations or have seen others go through an identical situation, we cannot honestly say that we know how this person feels. Rather we are wiser to say, "I cannot really know how you feel, but I want you to know I care—tell me about it."

Spending time with the dying and actually being there at the time of death not only benefits the one who is dying, but it can profoundly affect those present. It will give them a renewed appreciation for the value of life and may help prepare them for their own eventual demise. I am intrigued how few of my patients have actually been present at a death. No wonder they are apprehensive about facing their own. My mother's retirement community has a nursing home in the same building. Many of the residents who do not have someone who can be with them are moved to the nursing home as death approaches. There are a group of about eight ladies in the community who volunteer to "sit with the dying." I am very proud of Mom for being part of that group. She will sit with the patients, sing to them, massage their hands, and at times just be silent. She has seen death in many different ways, and when her time comes, she will be uniquely prepared.

Be Honest with Those Who Are Dying

The dying are often much more aware of impending death than their visitors want to acknowledge. How often have I heard a visitor come in to a patient who was clearly dying and say, "You look great!" I appreciate those people's desire to be encouraging and uplifting, but their lies are very shallow. How much better it would be to say, "I'm not sure how long you have to live, but I want you to know how glad I am to be with you now and how much I am going to miss you once you are gone."

Russian novelist Leo Tolstoy saw the importance of honesty and the tragic results of not being candid with the dying:

> What tormented Ivan Ilych most was the deception, the lie, which for some reason they all accepted, that he was not dying but was simply ill, and that he only need keep quiet and undergo a treatment and then something very good would result. He however knew that do what they would nothing would come of it, only still more agonizing suffering and death. This deception tortured him—their not wishing to admit what they all knew and what he knew, but wanting to lie to him concerning his terrible condition and wishing and forcing him to participate in that lie.[11]

Offer Hope

Earlier we discussed the importance of hope. Hope is important, even when death is very close. After the medical team has said that the patient will soon die, we still do not know how long it will be. After dealing with dying patients for years, I still can't accurately predict how long patients have to live. Over and over I have seen people live far beyond what was expected. Some even rally and do amazingly well for extended periods. We can offer hope day to day with confidence that our Lord will do what is right. We can also speak unhesitatingly about our hope of heaven. Ask people what they are looking forward to in heaven. What do they think it will be like? Read the end of Revelation. Read Romans 8 and continue to point them to their eternal future. Of greatest importance though, as we saw in strategy 2, is to remember our hope in God. He is strong, he is loving, and he will accomplish his purpose.

Share the Gospel

As Christians, we should always want to share the good news of Christ's sacrificial death with those who are dying, in the hope that even in their dying days they will respond by repenting of sin and trusting Jesus for their eternal well-being. The thief who died with Jesus did this within hours of death; so may all. If people come to the end of life and have never heard the good news that Jesus died for them, it is perfectly acceptable to share that with them. I have observed that one reason people resist the gospel in their healthy years is because they desire to be self-sufficient and independent. When death is coming quickly and people realize that soon they will stand before God, those who have heard the gospel may believe. The way I express it is, "When the plane is going down and there are only seconds to live, how many who have heard the gospel cry out to God for his salvation?" There are situations where people do not want me to share the gospel, but I have found that most people appreciate my offer to pray with them. It is easy to communicate the gospel when I pray.

Begin to Grieve and Plan

Anticipatory grief is the sadness we feel prior to the loss of a loved one. It is beneficial to be able to talk through these emotions openly. It must go both ways: the family should tell the dying how much he will be missed and how different their lives will be without him. At the same time the one who is dying needs to express how much he loves them. This is particularly true when death comes at a relatively young age. Dad needs to tell his daughter how much he is going to miss being at her wedding and seeing his grandchildren. Doing so will help her own grieving process. It is also helpful to discuss what life will be like after Dad or Mom is gone. How will the survivors be able to take over the roles that the dying has fulfilled? Different topics may need to be discussed. These may include finances, taking care of the house, and managing the myriad of things to be done after a death. For spouses such subjects as remarriage, handling sexual pressures, and raising the children are all subjects that may need to be addressed. It is tempting at this time to make rash promises (like never to sell the house or never to remarry), but this is not the time to do that. The key is that you acknowledge that while changes will come, both the dying and the survivors need to be assured that things will be all right.

Let Go

One of the most difficult things to do is to let go and allow loved ones to die. It is only natural for family to want to cling to them. The reasons are typically loving and good—for example, the fear of facing life without the steadying help of a parent. At other times the refusal to let go is less commendable, such as guilt stemming from years of neglect. It is not uncommon that a refusal to let go stands in the way of a peaceful and dignified death. I remember Lena, who was faithfully cared for by her daughter Jan for many years. Lena had terminal cancer and was in hospice. It was clear she was close to the end, and Jan finally convinced her brother Jay, who lived in California and had not seen his mother for ten years, to come for a last visit. When he arrived, Jay demanded that his mother be immediately hospitalized, stating, "I love her too much to just let her go." Suffice it to say, Jay did not get his way. Letting go is often best communicated by giving someone permission to die. At times terminally ill patients may hold onto life because they fear disappointing their loved ones. As a result, they may ask the doctor to help them stay alive even though they themselves would rather die. I have repeatedly seen a dying person relax and rest after being told by their family that it is okay to let go. People often stop struggling to breathe and die more comfortably than they might otherwise have.

Do We Get a Sense of Impending Death?

When deacon Stephen was being stoned to death (Acts 7), he saw a vision of Jesus in heaven. The apostle Paul related a near-death experience where the individual was caught up into heaven. This shows that God can give some a glimpse of glory even before they leave this earth. I have heard many people recount similar situations, and I fully believe them. This is a gift God gives to some, and then what a blessing it is! It is an affirmation of faith both for the dying and those nearby. My friend Carl wrote me several years ago after his wife, Betsy, died. She had endured a lingering, wasting death from inflammatory bowel disease and died in her early fifties. As she was dying, Carl took her in his arms. He relates that just before she died, she raised her arms and said, "Oh, Carl, it's so beautiful." Carl tells how much those five words have meant to him. They allowed him to feel more comfortable with her death and have motivated him to share the good news of Jesus with others in ways he never before would have felt comfortable doing.

Rest in Jesus

We come now to the moment of death. Here we have the final chance in this life to entrust control of our lives to the Lord. No longer do we need to do anything. Now we can simply rest in him. The fight is over, the victory is won, and we are able to enter our eternal home. We have said good-bye to the things of this world. Our attachments have been severed, and now we can confidently respond to his call and enter his presence. I am convinced that God is glorified when his children respond without fear to his calling them home.

God has promised to be with us when we die:

Even though I walk through the valley of the shadow
      of death,
   I will fear no evil,
for you are with me;
   your rod and your staff,
   they comfort me. (Ps. 23:4)

Now, perhaps as never before, we can treasure God. We will know the profound meaning of: "For from him and through him and to him are all things. To him be glory forever. Amen" (Rom. 11:36).

Conclusion

Our final strategy to finish life well is simple yet profound. It is our opportunity to rest in Jesus. Put the struggles behind; there is no longer need to think about what we can do, what we have done, or what we have failed to do. Now we simply take comfort in what he has done. He died to take the sting of death from us. We are invited to enjoy him and rest.

Prayer

Lord Jesus, this sounds so good; thank you for the salvation you give in Christ Jesus. Within me there is a great longing to trust you and find in you my peace and joy. But Lord, there is also great uncertainty. When my time comes, will I have the ability to experience this rest, or will I be struggling? Lord, I feel like the man who brought his epileptic son to you. He said, "I believe; help my unbelief!" (Mark 9:24). So it is with me. I pray that between now and when you call me home you will increase my faith so that I will rest in you. In this way I trust that my death will glorify you. Amen.

=== MEDITATION ===

My Jesus, I love thee, I know thou art mine;
   for thee all the follies of sin I resign.

My gracious Redeemer, my Savior art thou;
if ever I loved thee, my Jesus, 'tis now.

I love thee because thou hast first loved me,
and purchased my pardon on Calvary's tree;
I love thee for wearing the thorns on thy brow;
if ever I loved thee, my Jesus, 'tis now.

I'll love thee in life, I will love thee in death,
And praise thee as long as thou lendest me breath,
And say as the death dew lies cold on my brow,
If ever I loved thee, my Jesus 'tis now.

In mansions of glory and endless delight,
I'll ever adore thee in heaven so bright;
I'll sing with the glittering crown on my brow:
if ever I loved thee, my Jesus, 'tis now.

"MY JESUS, I LOVE THEE,"
WILLIAM FEATHERSTONE (1864)

Maintain Your Health

Maintaining good health is often the result of choices made earlier in life. We should consider several necessities.

Exercise

Perhaps the most important choice to make is exercising regularly. I received a card once from a good friend that quoted geriatrician Robert Butler: "If exercise could be purchased in a pill, it would be the single most widely prescribed and beneficial medicine in the nation." That is so right. We need to keep physically active to maintain our muscle strength, tone, and balance, which will translate into fewer falls and fractures. Additionally we will better control our cholesterol, blood sugar, blood pressure, and weight. Our bones will be stronger to further reduce fractures.

Exercise helps us maintain a proper emotional outlook and is a great stress reliever. Working out can be a social outlet if we do it with others; if you exercise by yourself, as I do, it is a means to practice solitude and enjoy some peace and quiet. I do not believe you can do much better than walking; but swimming, biking, aerobics, or activities like Tai Chi are also very effective. I recommend doing any of these three hours a week. It is helpful to complement aerobic activity like walking with mild weight training to help maintain strength and balance. Those who are active in hobbies such as gardening and other more vigorous activities get the exercise they need in these enjoyable pastimes.

If these reasons aren't enough to motivate you to exercise, consider the following statistics. We usually hit our maximal muscle mass at about thirty; we maintain it fairly well. But in our sixties, without special efforts to keep in shape, we start losing about 1 percent each year. In our seventies it is 2 percent; eighties, 4 percent; and nineties, 8 percent.[1] It does not take a math genius to figure out that without exercising, the elderly will not have much muscle mass left.

What about assistive devices? These include anything from canes to scooters. The important question is, "Will this device help you get stronger or will it make you weaker?" For example, canes and walkers may allow people to be more stable, walk more safely, and allow them to get more exercise. On the other hand, wheelchairs and scooters may cause people to walk less, making them weaker. There is still a role for these devices in allowing those who are confined to their homes to have more freedom to get out. But the benefits must be weighed against the weakness that may ensue.

Diet
All agree that our diet affects our health, but not on what a healthy diet should consist of. Yet adequate guidelines for good eating are not that complicated. There is no question that a diet low in fats and processed starches while being high in fiber, fruits, and vegetables is key. In addition, we should be sure we get enough calories to meet our needs, though not necessarily our desires.

We should also think sensibly about our need for supplements. This is a difficult issue since there are many more opinions than solid research about them. I feel that for anyone whose diet is restricted for one reason or another, a daily multiple vitamin is in order. There is also convincing evidence of the need for supplemental calcium and vitamin D. What we need beyond these is controversial. I see people taking huge amounts of vitamins and supplements who feel great and others taking similar things who feel poorly. The same is true for those who take none: some are robust while others are not. To those who attribute their well-being to the supplements they are taking, I like to tell the story of Ted and Ned. These were two friends who walked together each day. As they entered the woods, Ned would don a pair of oversized red sunglasses. After months of curiosity, but being afraid to ask, Ted blurted out, "Ned, why do you wear those hideous things?" Ned confidently replied, "Because they keep the elephants from jumping out of the trees on me!" Ted of course asked, "Come on now, when did that ever happen?" Ned's response was classic: "See how good they work!" If you are taking supplements, don't assume that they are helping you just because someone advised you to take them. Ask yourself if they are doing you any good. Be sure your physician knows that you are taking them for they may have serious interactions with prescription medications.

Preventative Health Exams
I recommend a yearly health maintenance exam after age fifty. These provide times to review any symptoms you may have, check blood pressure, sugar, and cholesterol, and allow follow-up of any abnormalities found. It is wise to review your health maintenance program and get suggestions for better diet and exercise. Your immunizations should be updated. Cancer screening has an important role for the younger elderly. After age seventy-five there is controversy concerning some of those screens, so you should discuss them with your primary care physician.

Good Medical Treatments
One of my great joys is to be able to provide medical care that allows my patients to be active in the service of the Lord. For

some this involves prescribing medications that lower cholesterol or blood pressure and prevent strokes or heart attacks. For others, this means referring them for hip or knee replacements to allow them to be more ambulatory. These have the additional benefits of preserving their ability to exercise and keep the rest of their bodies healthy. There are innumerable treatments available, and if they allow us to continue to function and serve, we should pursue them with vigor as good stewards of the bodies God has entrusted to us.

Preserving Intellectual Function

We see three categories of intellectual compromise in the elderly. First, we will all experience what has been termed "benign senescent forgetfulness." Some will develop dementia, most commonly Alzheimer's. Finally, there are those who have "mild cognitive impairment." These people are in the early stages of dementia and as yet cannot be distinguished from those with a more benign process.

Evidence shows that keeping the brain active will reduce forgetfulness, but doing so will have little benefit for dementia. Nevertheless, it is still wise to pursue intellectual challenges. Read good books and discuss them with a group. Do crossword puzzles and number games; enjoy cards and board games. Above all, do not sit and allow the TV to simply amuse you. Remember, the word *a-muse* literally means "no thinking." Treatment for dementia is in its infancy. Drugs available now can be helpful, but much more effective treatment will come within the next decades.

Examples of Technology

The technological options capable of significantly prolonging life are numerous. Whether to use these technologies or not is a common dilemma faced at the end of life. It is helpful to consider some of them in more detail in order to weigh their potential benefits and burdens.

CPR (Cardiopulmonary Resuscitation)
For millennia of human history, death always came when the heart stopped and breathing ceased. There were no options; you died and that was it. It has only been in the last half century that we have had the option of trying to keep alive someone who is imminently dying. A major means of doing so is CPR. Each one of us will someday experience cardiac arrest (when our hearts stop). Therefore CPR is the only technological intervention that could involve each of us. Our society has made the decision that CPR is the only medical procedure that is assumed to be done on

everyone at the time of death. Everything else done in medicine requires consent. CPR requires consent *not* to be done. The basic procedure is to first give a sharp blow to the chest in an effort to electrically restart the heart, then to physically compress the chest to allow the heart to pump blood. As soon as possible an electric shock is delivered to the heart by means of a defibrillator and intravenous lines are established to deliver medications. If CPR is successful, the heart can be restarted and circulation restored. If during the attempt the brain gets enough oxygen, it escapes without damage and the patient can resume normal life. The benefits of using CPR are enormous. One of my patients told me of his fifty-four-year-old son (a physician) who collapsed last week in the hospital with sudden death. He was immediately resuscitated by his colleagues and left the hospital in two days. He is taking two weeks off and will then return to work.

But there are burdens to using CPR.

First, it is not always successful. One study published a number of years ago showed that of one hundred cardiac arrest patients on a hospital floor who received CPR, seventy did not survive the attempt. Of the thirty who survived, twenty died before they left the hospital, and six of the ten who left the hospital were alive five years later.[1] The one place where the statistics are significantly improved is in an intensive care unit, where the moment the heart stops, it is recognized and responded to quickly. The context that has the greatest chance of CPR failure is in the community, including nursing homes. In those situations it all too often takes too much time to mobilize the team and equipment. In general the success of CPR depends on the number of other medical problems the patient has. If the patient is dying of another disease such as cancer or an overwhelming infection, CPR is rarely effective.

Second, if there is a prolonged period when the brain goes without circulation, there is a significant chance of major brain damage. The older the patient and the more compromised the circulation to the brain, the greater is this likelihood. I find that this is a burden that few adequately consider; but CPR is the most common cause of the type of severe brain impairment such as was experienced by Terri Schiavo, the woman who died so tragically in Florida in 2005.

Third, the act of compressing the chest can often break ribs, and using a defibrillator can burn the chest. These are small burdens compared to the benefit of restoring life, but for those who survive the attempt only to sustain another arrest, it can create much suffering in the final days or hours of life. I recall years ago when my uncle was resuscitated more than fifty times before he eventually died.

It is interesting to observe many people's perception of CPR. One fascinating study showed that, contrary to the numbers quoted above, the success of CPR on American television was 67 percent, while on British TV it was only 30 percent. Americans are given a rosy picture of the technology that does not correspond with reality. I recall to my horror being in a two-bed hospital room once, overhearing one of my colleagues, an excellent physician, discussing CPR with a patient. The doctor's question was, "If your heart stops, do you want us to start it up again?" Under my breath I groaned, and said, "I wish it were that simple."

For a number of years health-care facilities, including hospitals and nursing homes, have been required to ask one's choice for or against CPR on admission. That is a decision which must be made very carefully. In the proper context CPR is proportionate and good stewardship of our bodies. In other contexts it can amount to an effort to resist God's will, and it may compound end-of-life suffering.

Ventilators

Deciding whether to use a ventilator is another common and difficult choice that will have to be made for many of us. Ventilators require a plastic tube to be inserted either through the mouth or nose or by means of a small incision in the neck called a tracheotomy. The tube allows patients to be attached to a ventilator, a machine that will move air in and out of their chests and therefore breathe for them. The entire procedure can be most uncomfortable, and many patients require heavy sedation to enable them to tolerate the tube and the machine. Sedation often weakens them and makes it more difficult to regain enough strength to breathe on their own. The sedation plus the patient's inability to talk while on the ventilator makes communication very difficult.

This is why it is wise to carefully discuss the patient's attitude toward the ventilator as soon as it is recognized that one may be necessary. Does he want it, and if so, does he want to put a time limit on its use?

Dialysis

Kidney failure is an all too common complication near the end of life. At times it is the primary problem; in other situations it is a complication of another treatable disease such as diabetes or hypertension. Then there are times when it is a complication of untreatable disease or is part of a syndrome called "multiple organ failure." Kidney failure can be effectively treated by dialysis.

Dialysis can be done two ways. Most commonly used is hemodialysis, which uses the traditional kidney machine. Here the patient has a minor surgical procedure in the arm that allows the blood to leave the body, circulate through the dialysis machine, and be returned to the body. Less common is peritoneal dialysis; a tube is inserted into the abdomen through which a salt water solution is run and then drained out several times each day. Hemodialysis is occasionally done at home but much more commonly is done in a dialysis center, where the patient goes for about eight hours, three days a week. Peritoneal dialysis is usually done at home. While on dialysis, patients typically feel reasonably well and are able to live rather normal lives. But some people do not tolerate dialysis well; they have frequent complications and choose not to live under those conditions. When patients request that dialysis be discontinued, they typically go into a coma after about one week and die within a week or so after that.

Is using dialysis right or wrong? I feel that when it is used in the context of multiple organ failure, it is rarely justified. When it is in the context of an otherwise treatable disease, patients should give it a try.

Sam had diabetes for years. He had a stroke in his fifties, and later had several heart attacks. At seventy his kidneys began to fail and he needed dialysis. After extensive discussion, he refused it. As the kidneys continued to fail, Sam developed more complications and died struggling to breathe. I respect his decision to refuse dialysis since he did not want to prolong his life; but I also recognize that dialysis could have spared him some of his suffering at the end.

Transplants

One of the most exciting technological developments in recent decades is organ transplantation. This technology is much less common then those we have been discussing, but it raises so many questions that it is worthy of comment. In general, transplants are a gift of God. A lung transplant may eliminate the need for the long-term use of a ventilator. A kidney transplant prevents the need for dialysis. Surgical techniques are now excellent and surgical mortality is very low. The new antirejection drugs have fewer side effects and are more effective than ever. Therefore, whether we are talking about heart, lung, kidney, liver, or other smaller organs, the life span of the transplanted organ is quite acceptable and that of the recipient patient is even better. The benefits frequently far outweigh the burdens.

I am a strong proponent of being an organ donor. The concept of giving life to another, even at the time of your death, is a particularly Christian thing to do. In a spiritual sense that is what Jesus has done for us. In the case of a living donor, it is a worthwhile gift that we can give to another. I see no moral problems with being the donor or recipient of a transplanted organ.

Routine Treatments, Antibiotics, Medications, Surgeries, Etc.

Doctors make decisions every day to give medications and perform surgeries on people. Rarely do we consider the moral implications of them. When we do things that are fairly simple, cause minimal burden, and can offer benefits, patients generally have little trouble saying yes to them. Still there are times when people might choose to forgo these treatments. Whether we are talking about using antibiotics to treat pneumonia or removing an appendix, or using aggressive chemotherapy or performing open-heart surgery, the principles are similar. All of these interventions could be classified as extraordinary care, and are therefore not always morally required. However, if we think in terms of proportionate or disproportionate care, we can make wiser decisions. Generally, if the patient has a terminal disease and the question is not *if* but *when* he will die, and especially if he is in pain or suffering, any treatment intended to prolong life may be disproportionate. On the other hand if he is doing well and enjoying a high quality of life, it seems wise to pursue any reasonable available treatment.

Howard was eighty-six; his wife was demented and living in a nursing home. He was a retired missionary and often spoke of longing to be with the Lord. He had severe hardening of the arteries and had already had one leg amputated, and he was in constant pain from multiple pinched nerves in his spine. One afternoon Howard developed excruciating back pain and passed out. He was brought to the emergency room where a CAT scan confirmed the initial suspicion of a ruptured aorta. An immediate decision was required whether to take him to the operating room for emergency repair or to allow him to die peacefully. The decision was made not to do the surgery. He was given morphine for pain and taken to a private room where he died in the presence of his son several hours later. All involved felt that the benefits of surgery did not outweigh the burdens. Surgery would have been disproportionate, since the chance that it would have been successful was so small.

When Jerry was fifty-three, he was admitted to the hospital with a minor heart attack and serious heart rhythm disturbance. He was otherwise healthy. He requested that in the case of a cardiac arrest nothing be done to resuscitate him and said that in no way did he want bypass surgery. It seemed appropriate to challenge that request. In my mind the benefit of treatment far outweighed the burden. After discussion, Jerry changed his mind. Surgery did prove necessary, it was done and, Jerry is now in his seventies living a full life.

Artificial Nutrition and Hydration-Feeding Tubes

The choice of whether to provide artificial feeding and hydration is frequently one of the most challenging, in part because of the potential to provide great benefit with limited burden. The technique is to place a small (one-eighth inch diameter) plastic tube through the nose into the stomach for short-term use. For more long-term use the tube can be placed directly through the skin into the stomach. Rarely does that type of feeding tube require more cutting surgery. Highly nutritious liquid feedings, fluids, and medications can then be administered to the patient to meet her nutritional requirements. By these means life can be sustained for long periods.

Feeding tubes cause little discomfort, but they are not without their burdens. Diarrhea is a frequent problem. Because people who require feeding tubes are frequently debilitated, diarrhea can lead to serious bed sores. Sometimes feeding tubes may prolong a life of pain and suffering, making their use disproportionate. For the terminally ill, they may significantly increase the suffering of dying. Hospice nurse Deborah Howard wisely observes:

> Many people, including medical personnel, worry about dehydration. They push for IV hydration or tube feeding. This may sound harsh, but dehydration is a dying person's friend. It is one of the most peaceful ways to exit this world. Many times in the hospital, IV hydration is begun, but that can create fluid overload and bloating, adding to the patient's discomfort. If the circulatory system is compromised it may not be able to handle additional fluids. In most cases, the extra fluid goes to the lungs, and what follows is an unpleasant "respiratory" death. The patient sounds as if he is drowning in the fluid filling his lungs. In contrast, when a person

dies in a state of dehydration he just becomes weaker and weaker until he goes to sleep and peacefully drifts away.[2]

I find it curious that in much of the world when someone stops eating, it is considered to be a sign of impending death. Many in the Western world view it as the cause of death.

Personally, I do not have set attitudes about feeding tubes. Sometimes I recommend them and sometimes I do not. I like to use feeding tubes in situations where there is a treatable problem that temporarily prevents swallowing, when the patient or their family desire it, and when the feeding tube will facilitate a quality of life desired by the patient. I do not like to use feeding tubes when a patient is imminently dying, has a terminal disease where the feeding tube only prolongs the inevitable (including Alzheimer's),[3] or where it will prolong pain and suffering.

Whether a feeding tube is used or not, when a patient dies, the cause of death is the underlying disease. When a patient has a massive stroke and dies of complications of the stroke, that is the cause of death, not the fact that a feeding tube was not inserted to provide artificial feeding and nutrition.

At the present time feeding tubes are among the most controversial of all technologies. People often quote our Lord, who said that when we give food and water to those in need, we do it as unto him (see Matt. 25:31–40). The question is, was Jesus speaking of food and drink by mouth, or do we extrapolate that to feeding tubes? Committed Christians take positions on both sides of that discussion. Neurologist and bioethicist Dr. Robert Cranston writes of the need for sensitivity and mutual respect in considering feeding tubes.[4] I fully agree.

Cardiac Devices: Pacemakers and Defibrillators

I find that using cardiac devices is similar to using feeding tubes in the sense that they can provide a great deal of benefit with limited burden. Many lives have been saved by these little electronic wonders that can be placed under the skin of the chest and wired to the heart. Other than the cost (which for a new-generation defibrillator can be in the $50,000 range), the burdens are few.[5] They are therefore also on the fringe of the definition of ordinary and extraordinary care. There are many cases where they should be used, and one would question the wisdom of refusing them. On the other hand, because they are a product of technology, they may be considered optional and are not strictly morally necessary.

Eunice was ninety and dying of heart failure. She had had a defibrillator implanted three years ago, and on three occasions it shocked her heart and had evidently saved her life. Now, however, her heart was giving out. She was at home in her living room, her family had gathered, and I stopped by to ensure that all appropriate measures were being taken for her comfort. Suddenly we realized that if her heart stopped soon (as expected), the defibrillator would kick in and potentially restart it. The manufacturer was called, and it dispatched a technician who was able to turn off the defibrillator to keep it from prolonging the life of this dying woman. A potentially life-saving technology was no longer appropriate.

Advice for Survivors

After the death of a loved one, we often feel a variety of competing emotions. Deep sadness might be accompanied by a sense of relief, especially if the death was slow and difficult. People often feel these emotions in the context of total exhaustion. Yet at that very time when it is natural to seek solace in peace and quiet, survivors are immediately faced with difficult challenges. They will need to make some decisions even before the reality of their loss has set in, perhaps even while still being in a state of shock. Those left behind will be better able to handle these matters if they are aware of them beforehand.

Deciding about an Autopsy

You may be asked if you desire or will consent to an autopsy immediately upon the death of a loved one. This is not done nearly as frequently as in the past, but it still occurs, particularly in teaching hospitals that conduct valuable research. Autopsies are still very useful to confirm the cause of death, especially where there is some question about it. They can be particularly valuable when the autopsy would disclose that someone died of a problem that might be inherited or otherwise acquired by family members. It is not always necessary to examine the entire body; a limited autopsy can be done, which involves only the part of the body known to be affected. I do not believe there are any biblical principles that would affect one's decision of whether to consent to an autopsy. Sometimes local authorities such as a coroner or medical examiner might require an autopsy.

Donating Organs

At or shortly before the time of death, the question of whether to donate organs will often be asked. When the deceased has previously indicated a desire to be an organ donor, his wishes should be followed. It seems tragic when what might be the patient's last request is not honored. If one is a registered organ donor (often indicated on a driver's license), some states will proceed with organ donation automatically while others still require permission from the power of attorney or next of kin. Too often I have seen survivors ignore their loved one's wish to be an organ donor. When asked for their permission, sometimes a family refuses, saying something such as, "Don't bother me with that; I have too many other things on my mind."

Choosing Cremation or Burial

Usually the decision of whether someone will be buried or cremated is made before a person dies. Often the deceased will have expressed a preference or the family has an established precedent. Any number of issues may be involved in this decision, including geography, local culture, and finances. I know of no biblical reasons why one should prefer burial or cremation. Some believers have spoken against cremation because they believe the body should be kept intact anticipating the resurrection. I find this argument unconvincing, because whether one's body is cremated or buried, both will end up, as the Bible says, "as dust." Christians are free to do what they deem best.

Opting for a Funeral or a Memorial Service

It is a matter of personal preference whether to have a funeral with the body present shortly after death or a memorial service some days or weeks after the burial or cremation. Ideally this should be discussed with the dying prior to death. It is important to keep in mind four purposes of whatever type of service you choose: first, to allow loved ones and the community to celebrate the life of the deceased; second, to give closure to the death; third, to provide a clear proclamation of the gospel; and fourth, to aid in grieving. It is always helpful when the deceased has given some direction prior to death. I appreciated that, before my dad died, he had made it clear to Mom that he was to be cremated and that there was to be a memorial service. He chose not to give other instructions except that he wanted us to be sure that the service "is about the Lord and not about me." Those simple instructions made planning easier for us.

Fixing Blame

It is very easy after a death to look back and second guess what went wrong. Sometimes we blame ourselves: "If only I had called the doctor sooner" or "I should have recognized she was turning yellow earlier and gotten help right away." Or we blame others: "If only the nurse had responded quicker to the call light" or "the doctor should have put her in the hospital right away." Looking back and assigning blame promotes ill will and conflict, and any accusations usually have no basis. The truest answer we can give is that God called our loved one home. However, I know that some deaths are caused by negligence for which there may be legal culpability. Most, however, are not. If you do believe that there was true negligence that resulted in someone's death and the culpable party is a Christian, the biblical response is to seek the person out and discuss the issue face-to-face before you seek legal counsel. The Christian Legal Society provides a mediation service that allows believers to resolve these situations without going to court.

Promoting Family Unity

It is one of my goals when dealing with a dying patient to have the family walk away from the graveside arm in arm, loving each other. I certainly hope that happens when I die. If there have been quarrels or disagreements prior to the death, those involved should talk through them and reconcile as soon as possible. Recall the four things Ira Byock encourages the dying to say: "I love you," "thank you," "forgive me," and "I forgive you." Some of these things may need to be said within the family circle after the death. It is wise not to discuss financial issues or the resolution of the estate before peace is made.

Grieving

Bereavement is a universal experience. Grieving is not a fault or a problem; it is a healthy process. Cultures accept it as normal, creating mourning rituals to help people deal with death. Christians, like others, should expect to grieve, just as godly people in biblical times did. For instance, when devout men buried Stephen, they made great lamentation over him (Acts 8:2). D. A. Carson writes, "The Bible assumes that those who are bereaved will grieve and their grief is never belittled."[1]

When a fellow believer dies, our grieving experience is different from what non-Christians experience. Paul wrote, "But we do not want you to be uninformed, brothers, about those who are asleep, that you may not grieve as others do who have no hope" (1 Thess. 4:13). We must expect to grieve when we lose a loved one, but we do it in the context of hope: "For since we believe that Jesus died and rose again, even so, through Jesus, God will bring with him those who have fallen asleep" (1 Thess. 4:14). To tell ourselves that we should not mourn because our loved ones are in a better place is to miss the point of grieving. We grieve not because the deceased are among the blessed; we grieve for what they are missing on earth and for our own loss of their companionship and love.

Grief is complex; a death can trigger all kinds of inner conflicts and emotions. Much depends on how a survivor has been related to a loved one. Naturally, if the two have been very close, the grieving might be severe. John Stott reminds us: "However firm our Christian faith may be, the loss of a close relative or friend causes a profound emotional shock. To lose a loved one is to lose a part of oneself. It calls for radical and painful adjustments, which may take many months."[2] If one's relationship with the deceased was not close, the grieving might include regret over the strained relationship. In this case the loss suffered is one of missed opportunities. Adding to the complexity is the effect that gender, age, personality structure, and cultural norms have on how one grieves.

Practical Suggestions for Grieving

Do not deny your feelings. It's best to admit to yourself and others what you are feeling. We must be careful not to simply say to ourselves: "Don't be sad; I should rejoice." Rather, we should recognize our emotions and deal with them appropriately.

I have seen the negative results of denying one's emotions. June was in her seventies when her husband of fifty years died a lingering death to cancer. She said that she wanted to be strong, and continuously talked about how good God is. At the same time she was not sleeping or eating and started to complain of intense headaches as her blood pressure soared. She said that she was rejoicing so much in the hope of Christ that she could not cry. She was going into a severe depression because she would not let herself grieve.

Be honest with God. Spend quiet, unhurried time in God's presence. If you are feeling an impasse between you and the Lord, that is okay. Acknowledge it and cry out to God. Read the Psalms, where godly men did not hesitate to cry out to God. Balance these readings with meditating on the goodness of God. Focus on the cross, and ask God to give you a deep experience of his love. Talk with yourself, and remember God's promises as did the psalmist: "Why are you downcast, O my soul? . . . Put your hope in God, for I will yet praise him . . ." (Ps. 42:5, NIV).

Allow grief to fulfill love. After his wife, Joy, died C. S. Lewis found that for the first time he could love her in truly unselfish ways. That is a very profound thought. This may not happen immediately. In fact shortly after the death of a spouse it is possible to be totally consumed with your own loss. But, eventually, it is possible to move to the unselfish love that Lewis experienced.

Take control of your emotions, thoughts, and actions. Questions that beg for answers may crowd our minds: "Why did this happen now?" "Why didn't God answer our prayers?" "Why didn't I spend more time with him?" It's best not to simply push these questions into the back of our minds. Rather, we should reflect on them, study the Scriptures to search for answers, and talk with others. But we also need to recognize that we may have to learn to live with unanswered questions. The eventual goal is for us to acknowledge the goodness of God in all things. To reach that endpoint may take much time and healing. When your emotions well up, give them sway for a short time; it is okay to sit and bawl. Then take control and force yourself to get up and do something. That will help you rein in those thoughts and emotions. You will need to be careful not to wrongfully act out your emotions by "taking out" your anger on others or yourself. And you must not allow your sadness to cause you to ignore your health.

Spend time with others. Meet with a few close friends to share your pain and shed tears, but don't feel that you need to open your heart to everyone. Allow yourself to be with others just for fun and laughter. As time goes on and healing progresses, you will find you will spend less time in tears and more in laughter.

Continue to be active. It's normal for a griever to be excused from routine activities for a period of time. But eventually it's best to return to work and social activities. It's important to keep being active even when your heart is not in the activity.

Behaving in ways contrary to our emotions helps change how we feel. Some find it helpful to leave familiar surroundings and strike out independently. My wife's father died when she was ten. I was impressed that two summers after his death, Dorothy's mother took her three daughters from their home in St. Louis and spent several months in California. They lived together in a college dormitory while Mother took a course. This gave them time and space to build new experiences together.

Remember that grieving takes time, but it will come to an end. As with most things in life, people do not finish grieving overnight. I have observed that grief for a spouse or child takes a minimum of six months. Even in the context of a lingering death, when we might think we are well prepared and have already been grieving, it still takes a lot of time after the death. But in time the sadness will decrease, the disturbing thoughts will subside, and you will come to the final stage: acceptance. The emptiness you experience will never completely be removed, but it will no longer be your focus or dominate your life.

Suggestions for Those Ministering to the Bereaved

Don't be quick to give superficial answers to difficult questions. Sit and wonder with the griever. It's okay to ponder questions together even though many may not have an answer. Recall how Job's friends sat silently with him for a whole week. Share truth with those who are grieving only as they appear ready to receive it.

You may recall that I advised not to say to the family of the dying, "Let me know if I can do anything." That puts an inappropriate burden on them. The same goes for those who are grieving. It is better to look for something that needs doing and simply ask for permission to do it. That will be more appreciated.

Encourage the grieving to seek medical help if you suspect they may need it. Don't be too quick to suggest antidepressants, since these drugs do not ultimately *make* anyone better though perhaps they may *feel* better. In addition, antidepressants have the potential to derail the grieving process. Understand how important getting enough sleep is to emotional health. Whereas an antidepressant may not be appropriate, something to help sleep (at least for a short time) may be. If the grieving person is not sleeping for fear of being alone, it might be good to have someone stay with him overnight. But be cautious that this does not create an unhealthy dependency.

Recommended Reading

Byock, Ira. *Dying Well: Peace and Possibilities at the End of Life.*
New York: Riverhead, 1997.

> A hospice physician recounts numerous case histories showing
> the potential for growth as life comes to an end.

———. *The Four Things That Matter Most: A Book about Living.*
New York: Free Press, 2004.

> Dr. Byock demonstrates how to bring closure to re-
> lationships.

Carson, D. A. *How Long O Lord? Reflections on Suffering and Evil.*
Grand Rapids: Baker, 1990.

> A New Testament scholar discusses biblical perspectives on
> suffering.

Dunn, Hank. *Hard Choices for Loving People: CPR, Artificial Feeding, Comfort Care, and the Patient with a Life-Threatening Illness.*
Landsdowne, VA: A&A, 2001.

> Nursing home chaplain Dunn lays the groundwork for loved
> ones making difficult end-of-life decisions but finding it hard
> to "let go."

Feinberg, John. *Where Is God? A Personal Story of Finding God in Grief and Suffering*. Nashville: Broadman and Holman, 2004.

> An evangelical theologian relates lessons he learned firsthand through his wife's experience with Huntington's Disease.

Howard, Deborah. *Sunsets: Reflections for Life's Final Journey*. Wheaton, IL: Crossway, 2005.

> Hospice nurse Howard follows the dying of a fictitious patient, demonstrating how spiritual growth can accompany dying.

Kilner, John F., Arlene B. Miller, and Edmund D. Pellegrino. *Dignity and Dying: A Christian Appraisal*. Grand Rapids: Eerdmans, 1996.

> An anthology of essays dealing with a variety of end-of-life issues.

Kilner, John. *Life on the Line: Ethics, Aging, Ending Patients' Lives, and Allocating Vital Resources*. Grand Rapids: Eerdmans, 1992.

> Theologian and ethicist Kilner develops biblical principles for making end-of-life decisions.

Kübler-Ross, Elizabeth. *On Death and Dying*. New York: MacMillan, 1969.

> A classic in literature on dying.

Moll, Rob. *The Art of Dying: Living Fully into the Life to Come*. Downers Grove, IL: IVP, 2010.

> Journalist Moll roots this book in the tradition of *Ars Moriendi* ("The Art of Dying") and demonstrates how these principles first articulated in the Middle Ages are possible today.

Piper, John. *Don't Waste Your Life*. Wheaton, IL: Crossway, 2003.

> Pastor Piper challenges us to steward well the closing days of our lives.

Piper, John and Justin Taylor, ed. *Suffering and the Sovereignty of God*. Wheaton, IL: Crossway, 2006.

> An anthology written by Reformed evangelicals arguing that God not only allows but ordains suffering for our good.

Sapp, Stephen. *Full of Years: Aging and the Elderly in the Bible and Today*. Nashville: Abingdon Press, 1987.

> An excellent overview of biblical texts that deal with aging and the end of life.

Tada, Joni Eareckson. *When God Weeps: Why Our Sufferings Matter to the Almighty*. Grand Rapids: Zondervan, 1997.

> Tada with Pastor Estes relates Joni's tragic story while developing a strongly biblical theodicy.

Notes

Introduction

1. One may erroneously conclude that Paul is speaking of gain for himself. In the context of this passage, however, that is not his point. His focus is not on his own comfort or pleasure but rather on the increased way the Lord Jesus could be honored. See Vernon J. Steiner, "The Gospel, Salvation, and the Church's Mission," *Miqra* 8.4 (Fall 2009): 12.

Strategy 1: Live Well

1. Paul Harvey, as quoted in Richard Corliss, "Paul Harvey," *Time*, March 16, 2009, 22.

2. Richard B. Hays and Judith C. Hays, "The Christian Practice of Growing Old: The Witness of Scripture" in *Growing Old in Christ*, ed. Stanley Hauerwas, Carole Bailey Stoneking, Keith G. Meador, and David Cloutier (Grand Rapids: Eerdmans, 2003), 11.

3. "All these are empowered by one and the same Spirit, who apportions to each one individually as he wills" (1 Cor. 12:11); "But grace was given to each one of us according to the measure of Christ's gift" (Eph. 4:7).

4. Joni Eareckson Tada, "The Quest for Control," lecture given at the Center for Bioethics and Human Dignity annual conference, The Reproductive Revolution, July 1998, Trinity Evangelical Divinity School.

5. Edward P. Sabin, "Social Relationships and Mortality among the Elderly," *Journal of Applied Gerontology* 12, no. 1 (1993): 44–60.

Strategy 2: Let Go Graciously

1. C. S. Lewis, *The Screwtape Letters* (London: G. Bles, 1942), article 28. http://members.fortunecity.com/phantom1/books2/c._s._lewis_-_the_screwtape_letters.htm.

2. Charles M. Sell, *Transitions through Adult Life* (Chicago: Moody Press, 1985), 219.

3. Vigen Guroian, *Life's Living toward Dying* (Grand Rapids: Eerdmans, 1996), 21.

4. C. S. Lewis, *A Grief Observed* (Greenwich, CT: Seabury Press, 1961), 1.

5. Ibid., 38.

6. Portia in William Shakespeare, *The Merchant of Venice*, 4.1, http://shakespeare.mit.edu/merchant/full.html/.

7. Normally I would not go along with a suggestion that a diagnosis be withheld. Nevertheless, in this situation I felt it was appropriate since we had no confirmation of the diagnosis. The question of whether to move her to a nursing home is still on hold so long as she can continue to make it successfully in assisted living.

8. See Philippians 4:6.

Strategy 3: Treasure God's Love; Love Him in Return

1. A. Skevington Wood, *Ephesians*, vol. 11, *The Expositor's Bible Commentary* (Grand Rapids: Zondervan, 1978), 51.

2. D. L. Moody quoted in J. Gilchrist Lawson, "D. L. Moody," WholesomeWords.org, accessed September 22, 2009, http://www.wholesomewords.org/biography/biomoody4.html.

3. This is the point of Pastor Tim Keller's sermon, "Paul's Prayer for Experience," New York, Redeemer Presbyterian Church, Nov 11, 2007. Available at www.redeemer.com.

4. Rick Warren, *The Purpose-Driven Life* (Grand Rapids: Zondervan, 2002), 17.

5. Henry Scougal, *The Life of God in the Soul of Man* (Philadelphia: A. Bartram, 1805), 32.

Strategy 4: Grow through Adversity

1. D. A. Carson, *How Long, O Lord?* (Grand Rapids: Baker, 1990), 245. This is an excellent treatise on a biblical view of suffering.

2. John Piper, *Future Grace* (Sisters, OR: Multnomah, 1995), 65ff. This is an excellent demonstration of how dependent we are as believers on God's future grace, but how assured we can be of it.

3. This is the thrust of much of Jeremy Taylor's writing in *Holy Living and Dying* (London: George Bell and Sons, 1883).

4. Joni Eareckson Tada, *The God I Love* (Grand Rapids: Zondervan, 2003), 349.

5. From Nikolai Velimirovic, *Prayers by the Lake* (Grayslake, IL: Serbian Orthodox Metropolitanate of New Gracanica, 1999). Velimirovich, a Serbian bishop, spoke out against Nazism in the early 1940s. Because of his protests, he was arrested and taken to the Dachau concentration camp. See "Bless My Enemies," OrthodoxyToday.org, accessed September 28, 2010, http://www.orthodoxytoday.org/articles/VelimirovichBlessEnemies.html.

6. Jeremy Taylor, *Holy Living and Dying* (London: George Bell and Sons, 1883), 379.

7. Horatio G. Spafford, "It Is Well with My Soul," 1873.

Stategy 5: Embrace a Biblical View of Life and Death

1. Merrill C. Tenney, *The Gospel of John*, vol. 9, *The Expositor's Bible Commentary* (Grand Rapids: Zondervan, 1981), 119.

2. "And falling to his knees he cried out with a loud voice, 'Lord, do not hold this sin against them.' And when he had said this, he fell asleep" (Acts 7:60); "For while we are still in this tent, we groan, being burdened—not that we would be unclothed, but that we would be further clothed, so that what is mortal may be swallowed up by life" (2 Cor. 5:4); "For we know that if the tent that is our earthly home is destroyed, we have a building from God, a house not made with hands, eternal in the heavens" (2 Cor. 5:1).

3. Murray J. Harris, *2 Corinthians*, vol. 10, *The Expositor's Bible Commentary* (Grand Rapids: Zondervan, 1976), 348.

"What did Paul understand to be involved in being 'at home with the Lord'? To be sure, the Greek preposition *pros* (here meaning 'with') in itself simply denotes location. Yet when it describes the interrelation of two persons, it necessarily implies a fellowship both active and reciprocal (cf. *pros* in Mark 6:3: 'Are not his sisters here *with* us?'). In any case, since the phrase 'at home with the Lord' depicts the Christian's eternal destiny (cf. 1 Thess 4:17; Phil. 1:23), what is thus signified must supersede earthly experience where the believer 'knows' the Lord (Phil. 3:10). So being 'at home with the Lord' is a higher form of the intimate fellowship with Christ than the believer experiences on earth."

4. C. S. Lewis, *The Last Battle* (New York: Collier Macmillan, 1970), 183–84.

Strategy 6: Complete Your Agenda

1. This idea is roughly taken from the excellent book by Stephen P. Kiernan, *Last Rights* (New York: St. Martin's Press, 2006).

2. Jane E. Brody, "Tough Question to Answer, Tough Answer to Hear," *The New York Times*, March 6, 2007.

3. Augustine wrote, "It is only in the face of death that man's self is born," quoted in Michel de Montaigne, *The Complete Essays of Montaigne*, trans. by Donald M. Frame (Stanford, CA: Stanford University Press, 1976), 63.

4. Marcus L. Loane, *Oxford and the Evangelical Succession* (London: Lutterworth Press, 1950), 130.

5. St. John of the Cross in Matthew Levering, *On Christian Dying* (Lanham, MD: Rowman & Littlefield, 2004), 95.

6. P. Singer, D. Martin, and M. Kelner, "Quality End-of-Life Care: Patient's Perspectives," *Journal of the American Medical Association* 281 (April 28, 1999): 163–68.

7. Kiernan, *Last Rights*, 122.

8. Ira Byock, *The Four Things That Matter Most* (New York: Free Press, A Division of Simon and Schuster, 2004), 1; and *Dying Well* (New York: Riverhead Books, 1997), 140.

Strategy 7: Make Appropriate Use of Technology

1. Blaise Pascal, *Pensées*, in *Great Books of the Western World*, vol. 33, (Chicago: Encyclopedia Britannica, 1952), 203–4.

2. Pete Jaggard, "Advance Directives: The Case for Greater Dialogue," in *Bioethics and the Future of Medicine*, ed. John F. Kilner, Nigel M. de S. Cameron, and David L. Schiedermayer (Grand Rapids: Eerdmans, 1995), 257.

3. Whereas I practice traditional "allopathic" medicine, I recognize that God has given wisdom to many other professional healers as well, and I would not want to discredit the fine work that many of them do.

4. Daniel Chandler, "Technological or Media Determinism," at Aberystwyth University, UK, last modified April 11, 2000, accessed September 28, 2010, http://www.aber.ac.uk/media/Documents/tecdet/tdet07.html.

5. Joanne Lynn, *By No Extraordinary Means: The Choice to Forgo Life-Sustaining Food and Water* (Bloomington, IN: Indiana University Press, 1989) as quoted by Hank Dunn, *Hard Choices for Loving People* (Lansdowne, VA: A&A, 2001), 58.

6. Ibid., 63.

7. Julie Appleby, "Debate Surrounds End-of-Life Health Care Costs," *USA Today*, October 18, 2006, http://www.usatoday.com/money/industries/health/2006-10-18-end-of-life-costs_x.htm.

8. Dunn, *Hard Choices*, 7ff.

Strategy 8: Changing Gears from Cure to Comfort Care

1. First stanza of the poem, in Dylan Thomas, *The Collected Poems of Dylan Thomas* (1953; repr. with new intro., New York: New Directions, 2010), 122

2. George M. Marsden. *Jonathan Edwards: A Life* (New Haven, CT: Yale University Press, 2003), 29.

3. Pope John Paul II, "Euthanasia, Declaration of the Sacred Congregation of Rite Doctrine of the Faith, May 5, 1980" in *On Moral Medicine*, ed. Stephen Lammers and Allen Verhey (Grand Rapids: Eerdmans, 1998), 655.

4. John Kilner, *Life on the Line* (Grand Rapids: Eerdmans, 1992), 139.

5. Nancy Gibbs and Michael Duffy, "Ruth and Billy Graham's Final Farewell," *Time*, August 20, 2007.

6. Jane Brody, "In Cancer Therapy, There Is a Time to Treat and a Time to Let Go," *The New York Times*, August 18, 2008.

7. "Fact Sheet," Reclaiming the End of Life, citing Society of Critical Care Medicine, 2006, accessed March 20, 2009, http://www.reclaimtheend.org/fact_sheet.php.

8. Committee on Care at the End of Life, *Approaching Death: Improving Care at the End of Life*, ed. Marilyn J. Field and Christine K. Cassel (Washington, DC: National Academy Press, 1997), 45, http://books.google.com/books?id=9I2V8 IMj0vsC&pg=PA45&lpg=PA45&dq=gallup+poll+on+dying+at+home&source =bl&ots=PELOlxYhsB&sig=sBPj6TUbIG62Avg1hlE5A5tXSYU&hl=en&ei=W z3ESdbrLZG-M7-B5Rc&sa=X&oi=book_result&resnum=1&ct=result.

9. This point is made very well by Deborah Howard in *Sunsets* (Wheaton, IL: Crossway, 2005), 241.

10. Daniel Callahan, *The Troubled Dream of Life: Living with Mortality* (New York: Simon Schuster, 1993), 201–2.

11. Elizabeth Kübler-Ross, *On Death and Dying* (New York: MacMillan, 1969), chaps. 2ff.

12. Howard, *Sunsets*, 167.

13. From "Meditation XVII" in John Donne, *Devotions upon Emergent Occasions, Together with Death's Duel* (Ann Arbor: University of Michigan Press, 1959), 108–9. For digital version, see Project Gutenberg, accessed September 28, 2010, http://www.gutenberg.org/files/23772/23772-h/23772-h.htm

14. Joni Eareckson Tada, "The Quest for Control," lecture given at the Center for Bioethics and Human Dignity annual conference, The Reproductive Revolution, July 1998, Trinity Evangelical Divinity School.

15. C. S. Lewis, *The Problem of Pain* (New York: Macmillan, 1962), 124.

Strategy 9: Rest in Jesus

1. Oliver O'Donovan, "Keeping Body and Soul Together," in *On Moral Medicine*, ed. Stephen E. Lammers and Allen Verhey (Grand Rapids: Eerdmans, 1998), 224.

2. A more complete discussion of these events can be found in Deborah Howard, *Sunsets* (Wheaton, IL: Crossway, 2005), 168ff.

3. John Donne, "Death's Duel" (1631), http://www.readprint.com/work-3027/Death-s-Duel-John-Donne.

4. David Biebel and Harold Koenig, *New Light on Depression, Help, Hope, and Answers for the Depressed and Those Who Love Them* (Grand Rapids: Zondervan, 2004), 41.

5. Billy Graham, *Facing Death and the Life After* (Nashville: W, 1987), 66.

6. Sir Thomas Moore, quoted in Matthew Levering, *On Christian Dying: Classic and Contemporary Texts* (Rowman & Littlefield, 2004), 83.

7. Richard Baxter, *Dying Thoughts* (Grand Rapids: Baker, 1976), 113.

8. Oregon's Death with Dignity Act, 2007, http://www.oregon.gov/DHS/ph/pas/docs/year10.pdf.

9. This point is made insightfully by John S. Feinberg in *Where Is God? A Personal Story of Finding God* (Nashville: Broadman and Holman, 2004), 55.

10. John S. Feinberg, *The Many Faces of Evil* (Wheaton, IL: Crossway, 2004), 457.

11. Leo Tolstoy, *The Death of Ivan Ilych*, trans. Louise and Alymer Maude (West, UT: Walking Lion Press, n.d.), 56.

Appendix 1: Maintain Your Health

1. Richard Train, "Sarcopenia: As We Age Muscle Loss Occurs," EzineArticles.com, http://ezinearticles.com/?Sarcopenia:-As-We-Age-Muscle-Loss-Occurs&id=297128.

Appendix 2: Examples of Technology

1. David Schiedermayer, "The Decision to Forgo CPR in the Elderly Patient," *Journal of the American Medical Association* 260 (October 14, 1988): 2096–97.

2. Deborah Howard, *Sunsets* (Wheaton, IL: Crossway, 2005), 171.

3. The specialty boards for both neurology and geriatrics have position papers that do not recommend the use of feeding tubes for the demented.

4. Robert E. Cranston, "Withholding or Withdrawing of Artificial Nutrition and Hydration," The Center for Bioethics and Human Dignity, November 19, 2001, http://www.cbhd.org/content/withholding-or-withdrawing-artificial-nutrition-and-hydration/. This is a thoughtful treatment of feeding tubes, emphasizing both sides of the question and the need for loving attitudes toward those with whom we may disagree.

5. The huge costs of these devices raise questions of justice.

Appendix 3: Advice for Survivors

1. D. A. Carson, *How Long, O Lord?* (Grand Rapids: Baker, 1990), 121.

2. John R. W. Stott, *The Gospel and the End of Times: The Message of 1 & 2 Thessalonians* (Downers Grove, IL: InterVarsity, 1991), 92–93.

Index